Metamorphosis

"Practical Steps to becoming a New Creation"

David Hopper

(Self-Published)

Printed in the United States of America

Forward

Is it possible to grow grass on rocks?
Yes, it is. I can show you pictures from
around the world of this exact thing
happening; but when you consider *how*
this happens, you realize that it was not
an easy accomplishment. This book is
about moving people from point A to
point B, but the phenomenon of grass
growing on rocks is where I got my
inspiration. It is no easier to move
people from point A to point B than it is
to grow grass on rocks!

As a pastor, it is my job to motivate
people to do things that they may see as
impossible, even unnatural to them—
much like growing grass on rocks.
However, people are special, unique,
and different; and their goals, ambitions,
and passions are not all the same. The
goal for me is to point them towards
their God-given purposes for life; but like

growing grass on rocks, it takes strategic effort and determination to accomplish the "impossible" unnatural things. With God, ALL things are possible, and that is my motivation for writing this book.

When you want to move to a new level of accomplishment, you need to be someone who not only is inspired to do so but one who has an unyielding dedication to get there. It is a learned trait that very few master and most struggle with their entire life. I look forward to joining you on this mission of becoming all that God has called *you* to be while, at the same time, you inspire others to do the same.

Make sure as you read this book that you are coaching someone each month with the material contained in each chapter. As you coach and help someone move from point A to point B, you will find yourself growing, as well. What you learn should cause you to adjust your thinking and re-evaluate what you are doing in your own life as you seek God and His purpose for you. Therefore, I am suggesting that you take time to practice the material found in this book in your own life as you help someone else do the same.

Each month (or biweekly) you need to read and then apply one chapter of this book. This isn't the type of book you just want to read through and put on the shelf. This is an application book that only works through the implementation of the steps. None of these steps will be surprising or contain groundbreaking revelations, and most of what you learn will be things you already inherently know.

The key with this material is in the application. Although it doesn't take very long to read and complete the steps on an intellectual level, you must physically *apply* them for them to work. You have said "yes" to this process by opening this book, so God is doing something in your life already. He has given you a desire to help others and to be used on a deeper level. Perhaps it will be that monthly accountability in your life that helps you move into a deeper commitment to our Lord. He desires a relationship that goes deep and has an effect in every area of your life.

Enjoy this adventure! Don't stress about missing a few weeks here and there or being behind a week or two. This is a life-long mission. If you are growing just a little bit closer to God each day, you will end up at a destination that is far closer to God than you are today.

Table of Contents

Chapter 1

Know the Details

"If he can do it, why not me?" These are the words I said to my wife as I wrote a check to the plumber. My wife had pulled too hard on the faucet of our sink, unknowingly pulling against a line below that burst open a pipe and shot water across the kitchen. We ran in a panic to find the emergency shut-off switch to the water as the tide rose. Once the water was off and we had saturated every towel in the house in our efforts to clean up the mess, we called a plumber.

It was a Saturday, and most of the numbers we called didn't answer; but within fifteen minutes, we had a plumber at our door. He walked in, stuck some kind of clogging agent in the hole, and five minutes later handed me the bill. It was impressive work, indeed—not the plugging up of the clog, mind you—but how **fast** I could be handed a bill for over $200! I said, "That's it?" To which he replied, "It's Saturday. You're lucky someone showed up. I will be back Monday to fix the pipe." Upon hearing that he would be back on Monday, my mind was a bit eased about the bill—thinking that the real work would take place on Monday.

When he came back that following Monday and replaced the broken part in less than twenty minutes, he then handed me another bill for over $200. My frustration level was rising significantly as I questioned him about the first $200, but to no avail. Instead, I received a condescending lesson about a plumber's time and skill. Consequently, I reluctantly paid the bill, just happy for this catastrophe to be over.

When he left, I turned to my wife and said, "Never again will I immediately assume I cannot do something in this house. If this guy can do it in less than 20 minutes, certainly I can learn this skill." No offense to the plumbers of the world, but the guy who showed up at my house that day didn't give me the impression that this was brain surgery or rocket science.

Nevertheless, I have had more than one frustration in home repair since that fateful Saturday, but I'm still not going to shortchange the brain that God gave me. There are limitations to my abilities, of course, and I will concede that not everyone is created equally equipped to do all things; but I firmly believe that there are many skills that we can learn if we are only willing to take the time to learn them.

I believe that moving from point A (where we are today) to point B (where we want or need to be) in different areas of our lives is one of those skills that we can learn. I use the phrase "from A to B" because the possibilities are endless of where a person can go when they start taking the steps involved to get there. It could be a personal weight goal, a job performance goal, a new life-decision goal, a personal achievement goal, or a breaking-of-a-bad-habit goal. "Point A to Point B" will be the general term I use to say "all things are possible" if we have the right skills and the right coaching required to achieve that greater success.

These skills not only apply to us individually, but my focus in this book will be towards helping OTHERS reach their God-given potential. There will always be different levels of accomplishments and successes as we reach out to motivate other people; but helping others grow and become their best is a learned ability that is motivated by love for others—the second greatest commandment. Even when it seems that it is an impossible task to motivate another person to reach new heights—whether it is physical, spiritual, mental, or emotional—it is important to remember that anyone can "grow grass on rocks" if he or she is willing to be strategic in the way they apply the support and commit to the time needed to see results. Application always takes time, but time is a gift of love that we can give to others.

People **move** people. Sometimes it is through a song, a poem, a sermon, a dance, or in a myriad of ways. Sometimes it is simply through words of encouragement and celebration; but we are moved by another's passion in one way or another. When we try to explain why something has moved us to a better place, we often speak of strategy, vision, or powerful ideas; but the truth is that something inspired our emotions. We might talk about making behavioral changes; but when someone has touched our emotions within, those deep forces that drive and motivate us to do the things we do, that is when we are inspired to move forward.

There are a lot of programs in this world that center on behavior changes in people. In fact, lots of people are making a living on producing the next big thing that is going to cause a behavioral change in your life. The number of teachers, speakers, pastors, politicians, etc. who are making money simply by just addressing behavioral change is unprecedented. I could turn on my television right now (no matter the day or time) and find fifteen infomercials with products that claim to have the potential to change my behavior. In between those shows I can see thousands of commercials promising me a changed life if I use their product. Unfortunately, I have been suckered into believing some of these short-term quick fixes and wondered why the claims and promises did not prove true for me? What a disappointment and letdown!

Imagine a boat that has dropped anchor in the ocean. The anchor is deep below the ocean floor tightly wedged between some rocks. The ocean waves are going to be able to move that boat around from left to right, and it may even seem like the boat has moved a bit; but it is still anchored to the floor and not far from where it began. Basically, the boat is going nowhere. Until the anchor is pulled up from the ocean floor and the boat is moved to another place, there will be no change.

The question for us as we try to move people to better places in their lives is this: How do we get people to pull up their "deep anchors" of fear and doubt, along with all kinds of strongholds or walls of resistance in their lives and move them to better places? The anchors must be pulled up before lasting changes can take place, and that is where the real work begins. People are basically resistant to change; it's like growing grass on rocks, but it can be done. All along the way, there will be new problems, and each new problem brings with it new sets of fears, doubts, and resistance. Anchors will be dropped; but when that happens, we must start all over in the process of moving someone towards their desired purpose, success, progress, or whatever the goals may have been at the beginning. Eventually, if we don't give up, we will see change and results that can last a lifetime.

This process of movement begins with "knowing the details" of those you are working with. We as normal human beings have become accustomed to short answers. It is polite to say, "How are you doing," when meeting someone new; but it is a little weird to wait for a long answer. Let's look at the way Jesus interacted with people:

John 4:15-18 (NASB)

15The woman said to Him, "Sir, give me this water, so I will not be thirsty nor come all the way here to draw." 16He said to her, "Go, call your husband and come here." 17The woman answered and said, "I have no husband." Jesus said to her, "You have correctly said, 'I have no husband'; 18for you have had five husbands, and the one whom you now have is not your husband; this you have said truly."

The key to Jesus really connecting with this woman is the fact that He knew the intricate details of her life. I know what you're probably thinking, "Ummm, ya, but He is Jesus. Of course, He knows the details of her life. I didn't see Him ask any specific questions?" You are right, and I also appreciate the fact that you understand the power of Jesus to know all the details of your life. However, for the purposes of knowing how to move people, the point we must understand here is that we must know the important details of the people we are working with. We are not God, so we must ask a lot more meaningful questions to get to the heart of who people are and what makes them tick.

How are you doing?

This is a great question. You probably have gotten pretty good at asking this question. However, you may not be so good at listening to the answer to this question. We all need to improve on our listening skills. Therefore, I have another question to add to this that I think will contribute to better listening. When you ask, "How are you doing?" no matter how the person responds, a good second or third question to add is:

"What else?" or "Tell me more."

By simply adding, "What else?" we begin to break down the first simple answers to "How are you doing."

With the question "What else?" it is possible to go on in conversation for hours while learning a lot more about this person that God has put into your life. You must understand that God has a greater purpose for your life and the life of the one you are coaching. He also has a grand plan going on in the bigger scheme of things; and for some reason, He chooses to use us as a part of it.

There isn't one person in your life who is there by accident; you just must figure out why God put them there. Each person in this world is uniquely designed

by God; but nevertheless, we humans
are always trying to look like each other
or trying to clone other things. On the
other hand, God makes a design and
then breaks the mold. How is it that six
billion people can be on the same planet
and not one of them look the same.
Each one of us has a unique fingerprint,
voiceprint, palm print, eye, face,
personality, spiritual gift, talents,
ambitions, passions, and on and on with
things that are special in every single
human being on the planet. Only God
could do something like that, and to not
be cognizant of these unique features
that God has put inside of us is sad. We
need to take the time to first know how
God has uniquely designed us
individually and then proceed to learn
about the unique details of the people
whom God has surrounded us with.
Listen to how God describes His
creations:

1 John 3:1 (NASB)

"See how great a love the Father has bestowed on us, that we would be called children of God…"

John 7:38 (NASB)

"He who believes in Me, as the Scripture said, 'From his innermost being will flow rivers of living water."

John 8:12 (NASB)

"Then Jesus again spoke to them, saying, 'I am the Light of the world; he who follows Me will not walk in the darkness, but will have the Light of life.'"

John 14:12-14 (NASB)

"Truly, truly, I say to you, he who believes in Me, the works that I do, he will do also; and greater works than these he will do; because I go to the Father. "Whatever you ask in My name, that will I do, so that the Father may be

glorified in the Son. "If you ask Me anything in My name, I will do it."

Do you think He is serious about His creation? He loves His people, and we need to love each other as well. Begin to practice this technique of knowing the details in other people's lives—it is not a complicated skill. It is merely about asking powerful questions that can open good dialogue rather than closing the conversation. Here is an example of a good question that almost guarantees to close the conversation:

"Is this a good goal for you in life?"

It doesn't seem like a bad question because it is getting into important areas of a person's life and prompting them to go deeper towards setting goals. However, it also closes the conversation because it invites a "Yes" or "No" answer. Yes or no answers go nowhere. If you want to open a conversation and really hear the details, you will ask the question like this:

"What makes the goals you have set effective?"

It is the same question, but it requires the person to go beyond "Yes" or "No" and dig into the heart of the matter, perhaps bringing to the surface something that they didn't even know existed in their subconscious. You already know the stated goals based on the question you are asking; but even if you didn't know, this question would pull those out. Therefore, whatever the response, the answer will demand deeper thought and real soul searching to give an honest answer. It also will allow you to determine if the person you are talking to has set appropriate or attainable goals. Consequently, it may result in a re-evaluation of the goals this person has set and allow you to help them make a more effective goal at this time in their life.

Everyone sets goals, but why they set those goals and what they really want to accomplish in life is different.
Sometimes people have subconscious dreams, and they just need someone to help them define their dreams and articulate how they can reach their goals. God has made every person unique, and powerful question such as those I have listed below will bring out those unique qualities as you help those you coach to move from point A to point B.

"Where are you now?"

"How can I be praying for you?"

"What do you want to address?"

"How can we work together?"

"How can we maximize our time together?"

"Help me understand who you are."

"Tell me about your spiritual journey in life."

"How would you describe your relationship with God right now?"

"What wins can we celebrate in your life?"

"How are you doing personally?"

"What would improve our relationship?"

"What issues are truly important to you right now?"

"What obstacles or challenges are you facing?"

"How can I be praying for you?"

As you seek to know the details regarding the ones that God has put in your life to coach, these are all good opening questions because they will help to open honest dialogue between you and the other person. Good listening requires that you not settle for the quick answers that we have all become accustomed to in our busy hectic lives. Good listening is punctuated with good questions such as the following:

"What else?"

"Tell me more."

As the person you are talking to grows more comfortable and confident that you are not in a hurry to get away, he or she will continue to open; and you can then move on to a more powerful question that will take the conversation to a deeper level.

One question that we often ask when someone volunteers something that has happened to them is this: "What did you learn from that?" Although, at first glance, this may seem like a good follow-up question, it does not really have the potential to take the dialogue any deeper. Personally, I could answer that question in about one sentence. On the other hand, a more powerful question would be **"How could you have learned more from that?"**

This question stops a person in his or her thought process and requires that they go deeper into their experiences and think about how much more they may have learned. It requires that they pass up the more obvious answers to look for the things they may have missed. In this way, you will start to learn about the details of what your person really wants to experience in life and where they really want to end up.

Another follow-up question that sounds good at first glance is, "It sounds like you may be contemplating two different paths?" Again, although this question acknowledges that you are listening and motivates the person to listen to what they are saying, it still closes the conversation. Personally, I could answer that question in less than one sentence. A better question might be,

"What are some of the choices you see as you move forward?"

This is a powerful question because it opens the dialogue to include more than just two possibilities. Indeed, the one you are talking to might only give you an either/or answer; but, as you continue to question them with "What else?" responses, a lightbulb may go off in their head that tells them that there are far more choices than they realized.

For example: The person you are talking to wants to lose ten pounds, so they answer your question with, "I need to get a gym membership and/or eat less sugar." Those responses may sound good, but are they the only choices available to them? As you say, "What else?" they could answer, "Well, I guess I could get surgery?" Your dialogue might continue like this: You say, "What else?" and they answer, "I could eat less at dinner?" You say, "What else?" and they answer, "I could

run with a friend three times a week?"
Then you say, "What else?" and they
answer, "I could starve myself for a
week?"

Granted, not all the answers will be
good or even appropriate answers, but
you have opened a far greater dialogue.
With this kind of dialogue, not only do
you get to know the personality and
characteristic details of the person you
are talking to, but it also opens a whole
new world of possibilities to that person.
Thus, through brainstorming with
powerful questions, the goal setting will
go from feeling impossible to not only
possible but with many ways to get
there. The real beauty of this method is
that **all** the ideas came from their mouth.
If you, the coach, were to give them a
list of all the possible ways that they
might reach their desired goal, they
would always see them as *your* ideas.
People, in general, tend to feel and say
things like, "That wouldn't work for me,"

because everyone seems to think that their circumstance is so different that no one has ever experienced it before. By having them brainstorm their own possible solutions, they may start to visualize successful endings to their present situations. People may change outward behaviors with your ideas; but they will literally move anchors in their life with their own ideas.

Listen to the questions Jesus asked people:

Matthew 6:28 (NASB)

"And why are you worried about clothing…"

Matthew 16:26 (NASB)

"For what will it profit a man if he gains the whole world and forfeits his soul? Or what will a man give in exchange for his soul?"

Matthew 7:3 (NASB)

"Why do you look at the speck that is in your brother's eye, but do not notice the log that is in your own eye?"

Luke 6:46 (NASB)

"Why do you call Me, 'Lord, Lord,' and do not do what I say?"

Jesus asked probing questions that stopped people in their tracks and made them question the direction they were going. With one probing question, He could cause a person to re-evaluate his whole life.

We probably won't be able to ask questions like Jesus did, but we can ask **better** questions. We can help people to pull up the anchors that keep them stuck at point A and help them move on to point B.

Application:

The material contained in this book will require that you do some homework if you want it to have a lasting effect in your life or in the lives of those you coach. You cannot grow grass on rocks if you are not willing to put in the time to develop these skills. Here is what to do next:

1. Ask two people in your life if they will be your "guinea pig" for the next six months while you practice your coaching skills. Say something like this:

"I'm working through a new process that helps people achieve their goals. I need someone with whom I can practice the concepts. Would you be willing to meet with me once a month for six months? You can pick a current goal that you are trying to achieve, and then I will ask some questions to help you further that goal."

2. If they agree, have them sign the coaching agreement on the following page.
3. Then set up your first meeting day and time.

Do this with two people. Every person is uniquely created by God and each one will present a different coaching experience for you. In addition, although the goals that people set are similar in many ways, they will be uniquely different for each person; so, having two people to practice on will give you two completely different perspectives. Thus, you will be better prepared to coach on a regular basis by the time you reach the end of the process outlined in this book.

4. Once you have picked two people, ask someone who has already gone through this process to coach you through the steps. After each meeting with the people you are coaching, call your instructor and

tell him the highs and lows of that meeting and allow him to coach you.

5. Have your first meeting with the person you are practicing these concepts with.

At your first meeting, discuss what kind of relationships they have had in the past with a coach, counselor, mentor, etc. Ask powerful questions to see what they enjoyed and disliked about those previous experiences. This will give you a better sense of what they valued from those times and how they have achieved success before. You will also learn what they didn't value and take note of the pitfalls you may need to look for this time around.

In addition, take some time to understand yourself and what you personally bring to this relationship. What are your strengths and weaknesses as you work with others? What are some of your dominating strengths that you may need to restrain to assure that this process can better work? Take a few minutes to work through the following strengths test, spiritual gifts tests, and inventories so that you can better know what you are personally bringing to the coaching relationship. The better you know how you personally are uniquely designed by God, the more you will be able to positively add to other people's lives without distracting them from their progress.

Strength Tests:

http://freestrengthstest.workuno.com/free-strengths-test.html

http://richardstep.com/richardstep-strengths-weaknesses-aptitude-test/

http://www.learnmyself.com/Personality-Test#q1

Spiritual Gifts Tests:

http://www.spiritualgiftstest.com/test/adult

http://www.supernaturaltruth.com/SpiritualGifts/Spiritual_Gifts_Test.php

http://www.kodachrome.org/spiritgift/

Inventories:

http://www.humanmetrics.com/cgi-win/JTypes2.asp

http://www.personalitytype.com/career_quiz

http://www.outofservice.com/bigfive/

(Websites are subject to change and are not the property of this book. Take the time to put key words into a search engine to find the latest tests available.)

Ground Rules:

Be intentional in this process.

Set clear times with those you are meeting with.

Set clear expectations to why you are doing this and your expectation on them to take it seriously, to keep each appointment, and to work through the goals they have set for themselves.

Use the following session forms so that the process moves forward each time you meet.

Do not set goals for those you are meeting with but rather, let **them** set clear, attainable goals for themselves.

Do not suggest goals or give ideas. Instead, ask them powerful questions that will help them set goals and come up with their own ideas.

My prayer for you is that God will enhance what He has already created inside of you. You are already a beautiful, talented, and gifted creation of His, and this time of growth is about moving anchors in your own life to be even more effective for the kingdom of God. Through this time of helping other succeed, you will also grow in your relationship with God and see how God can use you to do even greater things.

Six-month agreement between

_____

and

_____.

We will work together to move from point A to point B in life.

The goal that you have set for this next six months is:

_____

_____

_____

_____

We will meet for one hour a month over the next six months to achieve this goal.

The time and day we will meet will be as follows:

Day of the month:

_____

Time of the day:

_____

Starting on this day:

_____

Ending on this day:

_____

I will be on time for all appointments.

I will call if I need to reschedule one day in advance.

I will commit to the goals set each month and work towards those goals each month.

Confidentially will be maintained for all these times together.

Personal Information:

Name:

_____

Phone Number:

_____

Address:_____

_____

Email:

_____

Other:

_____

Session # _____

Goals set from last time:

1.

_____

_____

_____

2.

_____

_____

_____

3.

_____

_____

_____

Current Wins this month:

1.

_____

_____

_____

2.

_____

_____

_____

3.

_____

_____

_____

Current Obstacles:

1.

_____

_____

_____

2.

_____

_____

_____

3.

_____

_____

Goals for next session:

1.

_____

_____

_____

2.

_____

_____

_____

3.

_____

_____

_____

Prayer:

Chapter 2

Celebrate the Victories

On December 26, 2004, a tsunami was generated by an earthquake off the shores of Indonesia measuring 9.1 on the Richter scale. The earthquake's epicenter was near Sumatra, Indonesia, and the resulting tsunami claimed more than 225,000 lives in eleven countries. It inundated some coastal towns with waves up to one hundred feet. Indonesia and Sri Lanka were among the hardest hit.

I remember this moment as if it was yesterday. In fact, I can remember in detail my feelings when Katrina hit, when 9/11 happened, when Joplin was annihilated by a tornado. It seems like once or twice a year there is a horrific event that kills many people very quickly in the world. The news of these things and many others in our recent history continue to tell us that life is but a breath. It is natural for us to always be thinking about the future and pushing hard to prepare for it; but at the same time, we must never forget that our lives can be over in the blink of an eye. A natural disaster, heart-attack, car accident, or something equally devastating could happen tomorrow, and many times we focus on the achievements we have *not* achieved instead of seeing the small victories we are realizing daily. We need to stop each day and take time to give God the glory for the small victories of that day.

One more night that we can read a story to our kids is a victory. A day in the office when we can make a co-worker feel special is a victory. Being able to walk or run an extra mile or lift another weight is an opportunity for celebration. Another few minutes studying God's

Word is a victory. Even having a chance to meet with someone and celebrate small victories with them is a victory.

Small victories may not seem like much, but many small victories add up to big accomplishments! As the saying goes, "the journey of a lifetime begins with one small step." That is why I am dedicating this chapter to encouraging you to take time in every meeting you have with someone to stop and celebrate the victories in their life, no matter how small they may be. As you celebrate small victories for those you are leading, you will create an atmosphere of acceptance and comfort for the rest of your time together.

Research supports the value of celebrating the victories of those we work and live with daily. Celebration has proven to be a morale booster in all kinds of offices, meetings, homes, and elsewhere.

"In seventy work teams across diverse industries, for instance, members who sat in meetings together ended up sharing moods – either good or bad – within two hours." (1)

"Nurses, and even accountants, who monitored their moods over weeks or even every few hours as they worked together showed emotions that tracked together – and the group's shared moods were largely independent of the hassles they shared." (2)

"Studies of professional sports teams reveal similar results: Quite apart from the ups and downs of a team's standing, its players tend to synchronize their moods over a period of days and weeks." (3)

"Leaders give praise or withhold it, criticize well or destructively, offer support, or turn a blind eye to people's needs. They can frame the group's mission in ways that give more meaning to each person's contribution – or not. They can guide in ways that give people a sense of clarity and direction in their work and that encourage flexibility, setting people free to use their best sense of how to get the job done. All these acts help determine a leader's primal emotional impact." (4)

"Coaching implies motivating, inspiring, taking people to greater heights. It is a directive process by you, a manager, to train and orient an employee to the realities of your workplace, and to assist in removing the barriers to optimum work performance. Coaching is high-level leadership; it's communicating the what, the why, and then helping with the how – whether behavioral or attitudinal. You push people and encourage them to push themselves to the highest possible performance." (5)

The research, therefore, can be applied to support our need to celebrate the victories of the one-on-one coaching of others toward to their desired successes and goals, as well. In this one hour of face-to-face sharing, we have the unique opportunity to treat people as the great creations of God that they truly are. What does God value more than anything else in this world? He values people!

Romans 5:8 (NASB)

"But God demonstrates His own love toward us, in that while we were yet sinners, Christ died for us."

John 3:16 (NASB)

"For God so loved the world, that He gave His only begotten Son, that whoever believes in Him shall not perish, but have eternal life."

1 Peter 3:18 (NASB)

"For Christ also died for sins once for all, the just for the unjust, so that He might bring us to God, having been put to

death in the flesh, but made alive in the spirit;"

God values people! God values you and me more than anything else in this world. If God values us enough to die for our sins, perhaps we should also strive to see people the way God sees them—as having worth and value. We don't see God talking about great sermons, or speeches, or buildings, or metrics, or goals. We don't even see him talking about His own successes and results. Instead, over and over throughout scripture we see God talking about the value of people.

You can take this a step further by thinking about what has influenced you individually throughout your own history. What were the life-changing sermons in your life? Think of the top five speeches that changed your life? Or what were the buildings that moved you? The chances are that you might think of a few; you might even have some euphoric moments in your life when you achieved a goal such as earning a college degree or when you reached a benchmark that you had set for yourself.

However, even though these accomplishments might have changed your life to some degree, they pale in comparison to the impact that actual human beings have had in your life. For the most part, it was not the material things or goals that had the ability to motivate you; it was, rather, the impact of other people who had the capacity to change you, mold you, and guide you towards becoming the person you are today—for good or bad.

Furthermore, even if you could think of an incredible sermon that moved you to make a life change, what comes to your mind first? Is it some life-changing message you heard, or is it a life-changing person or people who have made a difference for you?

God values people more than anything. He spoke often of the value of people, His creations; and we need to value them as the life-changing beings that they are. Therefore, because people are so valuable, it is important that you do your best to help move the ones you coach to new heights of effectiveness as you celebrate the victories that God is doing daily in their lives.

As you meet with the person you are trying to move from point A to point B this month (or bi-monthly), do the following:

1. Spend 10 minutes—Know the Details
2. Spend 15 minutes—Celebrate the Victories
3. Then move to the worksheet at the end of this chapter.

No two people are alike in this world. God has uniquely created each person with a special purpose in this world.

Although people try to look like each other, act like each other, and even clone each other, God does not do that. Even when He creates identical twins, He gives them different personalities and characteristics, as well as identifying marks that make them uniquely different from one another. God makes each person and then breaks the mold to never be used again. We look different, we have unique fingerprints, handprints, voiceprints, personalities, spiritual gifts, talents and so much more, including God's purpose for our life. No matter how frustrating a person may be to work with, they are still a unique creation of God; and we can help them find God's unique purpose for their life.

It saddens me that so many people will live this life having never known the reality of finding their purpose for being here. Therefore, even if it feels like you are trying to "grow grass on rocks", you must do your best to never let those with whom you interact to miss this reality. Each person is a unique creation, and you can help them towards realizing their purpose in life by celebrating the victories of what God is doing in their life.

There have been times when I'm watching a professional team play that I have wondered what the point of the coach is. Why are they paying these individuals millions of dollars to stand on the sideline and yell commands to their teams? My initial thinking goes something like this: "Isn't the coach just some person who wasn't good enough to play on the team, so they decided to coach?" But then the coach calls for a timeout. Things are getting out of control, a crucial moment in the game is taking place, the team is starting to stray away from the game plan, so the coach calls timeout. This person, the coach who I didn't give much credit to initially, has thirty seconds to remind the team of its goal. This person has thirty seconds to draw up one play to win the game. This person has thirty seconds to get the team back on track. This one person has the responsibility and ability to motivate an entire team on to the celebration of a victory. That is when I realize why this person is paid so much money; they earn every dollar in those thirty seconds.

In the same way, you can also be the motivating factor behind someone achieving a victory in their life. It doesn't take long to motivate someone to see the finish line, and it doesn't take long to celebrate the victories along the way. You can be the difference of whether a person moves from point A to B—or not.

We need to celebrate the victories!

2 Peter 3:9 (NASB)

The Lord is not slow about His promise, as some count slowness, but is patient toward you, not wishing for any to perish but for all to come to repentance.

Ephesians 2:4-10 (NASB)

But God, being rich in mercy, because of His great love with which He loved us, even when we were dead in our transgressions, made us alive together with Christ (by grace you have been saved), and raised us up with Him, and seated us with Him in the heavenly places in Christ Jesus, so that in the ages to come He might show the surpassing riches of His grace in kindness toward us in Christ Jesus. For by grace, you have been saved through faith; and that not of yourselves, it is the gift of God; not as a result of works, so that no one may boast. For we are His workmanship, created in Christ Jesus for good works, which God prepared beforehand so that we would walk in them.

Read those verses again with the idea of God rejoicing over the victories in your life. His great love for us makes us alive! He is going to show us incredible kindness and grace. You are saved by His grace, so relax and enjoy the gift that is Jesus Christ in this world. This is a gift, not something you can earn, so stop trying to earn it. You are the workmanship of God, prepared for good things! Remember these victories in your life and celebrate them with others.

The last time you met with the people you are coaching and trying to help move from point A to point B, you had them set some goals. Now, the next time you meet with them, be sure to celebrate their successes by asking some powerful questions:

What were some of the key things you learned this last month about your goals?

What did you learn about your goals that were more urgent in your life?

What are some of the priorities you have about your goals?

What are some of the victories you had in the goals you made?

If you could improve just one area of your life or ministry, what would it be?

And don't forget the powerful question you learned in Chapter One— **"What else?"**

As you listen to the answers to these questions, you will have to determine which issues are truly important. Be careful that your meeting does not get hijacked by urgent issues, real or imagined. These are the day-to- day happenings that pop up, those issues that seem to be the center of the universe now but don't have anything to do with the long-term goals that have been set. Some urgent issues may go with the current goals and may need to be addressed; but if an urgent issue has nothing to do with the goals set in the first session, you will have to remind them to stay focused on the goals they have personally set. Therefore, it is a good idea to begin each time together by reminding them of the goals they have set—the goals that will move them from where they are to where they want to be.

If the urgent issue of the moment continues to hijack the meeting, you may have to ask, **"What are you willing to sacrifice in order to reach your goals?"**

This is a powerful question, and it has the potential to get the meeting back on track. At the same time, remind the person of what victories they have realized and take the time to celebrate those successes. You might ask how that victory was a step forward towards their goal. Then capitalize on that victory by proceeding to outline the next steps they need to take towards reaching their desired goal or goals.

Use the following form to "Celebrate the Victories" with the person you are meeting and coaching with towards moving from point A to B.

On the Road to Victory

What are your spiritual gifts?

1.

_____

2.

_____

3.

_____

What are your talents?

1.

_____

2.

_____

3.

_____

What current victories are you
experiencing?

1.

_____

2.

_____

3.

_____

How do you like to serve at church and
in the community?

1.

_____

2.

_____

3.

_____

If you knew you could not fail, what would you do for the glory of God?

_____
_____
_____
_____
_____

How are your current victories helping you on the road to victory?

_____
_____
_____
_____
_____
_____
_____
_____

What kept you from victory this month?

_____

_____

_____

_____

_____

_____

_____

What would have been a victory this last month?

1.

_____

2.

_____

3.

_____

What obstacle kept you from those victories?

1.

_____

2.

_____

3.

_____

What are 3 steps to get to the next victory?

1.

_____

2.

_____

3.

_____

Who are some people that can help you get to that victory?

1.

_____

2.

_____

3.

_____

When will you call them?

_____

_____

_____

How will you reward yourself when this happens?

_____

_____

_____

_____

_____

What will you stop doing to make this a priority?

_____

_____

_____

_____

_____

Research Bibliography

1. Work teams share moods: C. Bartel and R. Saavedra, "The Collective Construction of Work Group Moods," *Administrative Science Quarterly* 45 (2000): 187-231.

2. Nurses and accountants tracking moods: Peter Totterdell et al., "Evidence of Mood Linkage in Work Groups," *Journal of Personality and Social Psychology* 74 (1998): 1504-1515.

3. Sports teams: Peter Totterdell, "Catching Moods and Hitting Runs: Mood Linkage and Subjective Performance in Professional Sports Teams," *Journal of Applied Psychology* 85, no. 6 (2000): 848-859.

4. The leadership ripple effect: See Wallace Bachman, "Nice Guys Finish First: A SYMLOG Analysis

of U.S. Naval Commands," in The SYMLOG Practitioner: *Applications of Small Group Research*, ed. Richard Brian Polley, A. Paul Hare, and Philip J. Stone (New York: Praeger, 1988).

5. The leader's emotional impact in work groups: Anthony T. Pescosolido, "Emotional Intensity in Groups" (Ph.D. diss., Department of Organizational Behavior, Case Western Reserve University, 2000).

Chapter 3

Push Through the Noise

In Acts Chapter 20, Paul is talking to groups of people first in Macedonia and then in Greece. After being in Greece for three months, he learns that the Jews in that area are plotting against him, so he knows that he must move on. I can't imagine how Paul must have felt knowing that there were those who wanted to see him hurt or even dead; personally, I would have been discouraged that my words about Christ were causing people to want to bring me harm. I'm sure that a part of me would be tempted to question whether I had heard Jesus correctly when He called me to that ministry. I'm willing to take the difficult path that God has called me to do; but when there are people who would rather see me dead, I think that I might step back and re-evaluate the call.

We have a tendency in our modern-day faith to think that God's call is confirmed when the path includes all the right doors opening for us. Therefore, we pray for doors to open; but if that doesn't happen in the way we envisioned, we change our path; and to the modern ear, this strategy may sound good.
However, I'm not so sure that that is the example we are shown in the Bible because there are too many stories and experiences described and recorded that show something very different.

In Acts, we read about the many struggles, closed doors, death threats, beatings, and other setbacks that Paul faced as he continued to push forward, knowing that he was doing exactly what God had called him to do. Everything he faced was just so much "noise" to detract him from the path he was on, but his choice was to persevere and push through the noise on the way to fulfilling his purpose for God. Obviously, on the other hand, we have to be careful that we aren't blindly plowing through what we think is the "right" path when, in fact, it might be the wrong path for us; but when we have clearly heard God calling us to do something and then carefully set the goals needed to accomplish that call, we should not abandon that call just because it gets difficult.

Paul had his share of difficult, even frightening, moments throughout his ministry. One example is recorded regarding a sermon he preached when he was in Troas after he had gone back to Macedonia. This sermon is notable because it was very long, so long that it went past midnight and into the morning hours. One fellow attending that service was a guy named Eutychus who falls asleep from his third-floor window perch and plunges to his death. You can only imagine the chaos and alarm that such a tragedy would cause in any congregation; and I'm sure that that sermon ended abruptly! Paul in that moment probably was tempted to question not only his speaking style but whether he was even doing the right thing. However, if he did have those thoughts, he didn't allow them to stop him from pressing on. Instead, he pushes through the noise, embraces the young man, and brings him back to life. Consequently, he gets to experience one of the great miracles of the Bible because he trusted God even when the circumstance looked completely devastating. He pushes past what must have been overwhelming noise—crying in the street, gasps from the crowd, chaotic screams of fear—all to witness a miracle from God.

Paul then gets in a boat and pushes towards Jerusalem in hopes of being there on the day of Pentecost. He says to the group in Ephesus:

Acts 20:24-27 (NASB)

"But I do not consider my life of any account as dear to myself, so that I may finish my course and the ministry which I received from the Lord Jesus, to testify solemnly of the gospel of the grace of God...for I did not shrink from declaring to you the whole purpose of God."

This is the picture of a man who is pushing past all the noise that surrounds his life so that he can stay on the path that God has called him to. After several stops along the way, Paul ends up at the house of Philip the evangelist. While he is there, a prophet named Agabus takes Paul's belt, binds his feet and hands, and says, *"The Jews at Jerusalem will bind the man who owns this belt and deliver him into the hands of the Gentiles."* (Acts 21:11 NASB)

It is at this point that Paul experiences the "noise" of sincere concern for his life. "Noise" can come in all kinds of ways; it can be in the shape of criticism and negative setbacks of all kinds, but it can also come in the form of fear and concern for the path you have chosen. In this case, those in Philip's house once again beg him not to go on to Jerusalem; but Paul knows what God has called him to do, and he pushes past the noise of concern to do fulfill the purpose for which he was called.

The Bible is full of stories about men and women who knew what God had called them to do and pushed beyond all the noises to accomplish those goals. We must take notice of these examples and understand that it will not be easy to accomplish the missions that God has called us to. What are you willing to give up fulfilling what God has called you to do? What obstacles will you push past to achieve those goals?

What are the "noises" that you have had to overcome in your own life? Think about when you first accepted Christ into your life. Who were the people telling you that religion is full of hypocrites who don't understand science? How much did the things or people from you past cry out for you to return to a life that may have seemed easier? Consequently, what did you have to change in your life because you had made a choice and commitment to live differently? Of course, I am assuming that you have accepted Christ into your life and made the decision to live differently. However, I would be surprised if you are using this book to help you coach someone else in their life journey if you didn't already have a Biblical worldview. Nevertheless, if you haven't made that decision, what are the "noises" that keep you from doing so?

I am also assuming that, in retrospect, the "noises" you experienced before accepting Christ may have seemed easier than the ones you now experience. Most likely, they were not easy at all. Wasn't the noise deafening that tried to convince you that Christianity would be much harder to live? The "noise" may have come in the form of objections from a family with a completely different way of life. The "noise" may have come in the form of restrictions from a workplace that doesn't respect Christian values. The "noise" may have come in the form of resistance from a spouse who does not share your views about God. Noise is everywhere; and just when you have overcome one form of "noise," it will come against you in another.

Therefore, knowing that you face your own "noise" challenges, you will be able to empathize with those you are trying to help. As you meet with the person who has asked you to coach them from point A to point B, you may have to remind them to push beyond the "noises" in their life. As they bring up obstacles and struggles, and all the reasons that they cannot do what they should be doing, take a moment to ask them these important questions:

What are you willing to give up to accomplish your goals?

What obstacles will you have to push past to achieve these goals?

….and be sure to ask, "What Else?"

These questions serve as good reminders that powerful worthwhile goals sometimes require great sacrifice. When it comes to setting goals or embarking on obeying a call from God, people can be excited until they hit the first set of obstacles. Once they realize that they will have to sacrifice something, or when they discover that the price is higher than they thought, there is usually a lot of second-guessing and temptation to run away from the original goals.

The time of second-guessing and counting the cost is when a person needs to use discernment to judge whether the goal they want to set is really something they want to pursue or whether the call they feel is truly from God. Sometimes it is wise to direct a person to step back and recognize that not every goal is the best thing for them at the time and not every call is from God; but, with that being said, we also need to challenge people to recognize the "noises" of self-doubt and fear that get in the way of them moving forward.

As you meet with the person you are trying to move from point A to point B this month (or bi-weekly), do the following:

1. Spend 10 minutes—Know the Details
2. Spend 10 minutes—Celebrate the Victories
3. Spend 15 minutes—Push through the "noises" as you discuss the

current obstacles that are slowing down this process.

4. Then move on to the worksheet located at the end of this chapter.

In addition, when you take on the responsibility to coach another person to their successes, it is important for you to also realize that you will have to make some sacrifices, as well. Your sacrifices include your time, your patience, and your personal effort that has to be invested into someone who may not always seem to be making any progress. It can be very discouraging to work with someone who so quickly forgets the goals they set at the previous meeting. However, you must remember that you have been called to invest into this person at this time; and it is pleasing to God. It is God's commandment that we love Him and love others; and this is one of the best ways that we show love to others—

investing ourselves into other people's lives.

There will be distractions, not only for the person you coach but for yourself, as well. Not only must you help your person stay focused on their goals, but you also must stay focused on the original goals that you helped them set. By staying focused and shutting out the distracting "noises," you will be helping people do greater things for God, grow closer to God, and achieve God-sized goals in their lives. In the meantime, you will realize those same things happening in your own life!

It is important in this aspect of "growing grass on rocks" for you to remember the power of idea creation. People are bombarded by noise daily. Think about how many times you look at your phone throughout the day. How many times do you check email, voicemail, listen to the radio, watch TV, read magazines, peruse the Internet, or read a good book? We are all on data overload; and amid all that, it seems that everyone is trying to tell us their ideas or what they think is best for us all day long. Consequently, out of what we personally experience ourselves, it is easy to do the same to those that we coach. You may want to give advice and input your own ideas of what you think is best for your person, but that just becomes another form of "noise" that gets in the way of their progress.

It has long been proven that the ideas that come from the ones you coach will have far more sticking power. When the idea comes from their own mouths, the idea will not have the effect of just another voice telling them what they should do. Rather than being distracted, they will be revitalized and energized towards reaching their goals. You can confidently remind them that the goals they came up with from the beginning were their ideas, not yours.

Thus, it is important to keep this powerful question before them:

What will you do to achieve your goals?

What obstacles will you have to push past to achieve those goals?

What are you willing to give up in life to achieve those goals?

What reward will you give yourself when you achieve your goals?

You want to capture their imagination of how great that moment will be when they realize their goal! You do this by making them a stakeholder in the goal. Give them control of the idea, and the ability to achieve and overcome obstacles to get there will naturally follow.

Having said all of that, it will not always be an easy road to reaching a goal. It will take some brainstorming sessions to help the people you coach to push past the current noises that may be distracting them. As you lead people towards reaching a goal, you need to help them develop an organized plan of action that will fit their unique personality, spiritual giftedness, and talents. (Mind-mapping is another good tool to use. You can check out an example of mind-mapping at the end of this chapter.)

A good plan of action will connect them to the Who? What? How? When? And Cost? A good plan of action will have measurable goals along the way and agreed upon realistic steps to get there. Remember that you are not the only accountability partner for a person. Help them identify who else in their lives can hold them account table for reaching their goals.

I recommend that you use the following action planner to help move someone past the distracting noises in their life to refocus on the goals they have set for themselves:

Push Past the Noise!

S.M.A.R.T. Goals:

Specific

Measurable

Achievable

Related to your vision.

Timeframe

What is your **specific** goal?

_____

How will you **measure** your success?

_____

What are some of the **achievable** baby steps along the way?

_____

How are these goals **related** to God's vision for your life?

_____

What is your **timeframe** to accomplish these goals?

_____

How will you reward yourself when you accomplish these goals?

_____

Who will keep you accountable in these goals?

_____

What will you give up to accomplish these goals?

_____

What will be some of the obstacles you will have to overcome?

_____

How can you defeat these obstacles?

_____

If the answers are not coming quickly to the questions above, here are some Powerful Questions to ask in this process:

·	Describe your ideal vision for your life.

·	What obstacles could prevent you from realizing this vision?

·	How have you seen others achieve these goals?

·	What's an out-of-the-box way you could achieve this goal?

·	What are ten more ways to accomplish this goal?

· What are you willing to give up to accomplish these goals?

· How will you encourage and motivate others to share your vision and

goals?

· What can you delegate to others in these goals?

· How will you measure your progress?

· Who can help you stay on track with these goals?

· How would you like to be held accountable?

"What Else?"

Mind-Mapping Exercise

Chapter 4

Build the Target

One of the secrets to life that most people don't understand is that the future is something that is created; you build it with every action and life decision. Understand that I'm not talking about God's future for this world or the ultimate plan for the universe; rather, I'm talking about the small every-day decisions that we make, decisions that will determine our immediate and ultimately our long-range future. A quote I once heard by a man named John Richardson went like this: "When it comes to the future, there are three kinds of people: those who let it happen, those who make it happen, and those who wonder what happened." In this chapter, I want to address the subject of how every choice you make affects your future and how you will get this message across to the ones you coach as you try to move them from point A to point B?

As a leader, you will have to help the person you are investing your time and effort into to understand that they can change their future. They don't have to just let life happen to them or wonder how they got to where they are; they can make goals and set them come to fruition. The key, however, will be in how they plan to take the necessary steps and measurable benchmarks required to reach their target goals.

I am using the word "target" to describe a clear and precise destination of something that your person wants to see come to pass in their future. In one passage from the Bible, this target is described as the "prize" that God has put before us—our high calling.

Philippians 3:14 NIV

*I press on toward the goal to win the **prize** for which God has called me heavenward in Christ Jesus.*

This vision of a better future, or the prize that God has set before them to accomplish, should motivate them to set clear guidelines on how they will get there. If this picture is painted strong enough and the vision is clear enough, there will be a persistent and relentless pursuit to the targeted finish line.

Listen to those in the Bible who had a clear target and pursued it to completion:

Joshua 1:5-9 (NASB)

First, God gives a powerful vision in verse 5:

"No man will be able to stand before you all the days of your life. Just as I have been with Moses, I will be with you; I will not fail you or forsake you. "Be strong

and courageous, for you shall give this people possession of the land which I swore to their fathers to give them.

Then, God gives him a vision of how to get there in verse 7:

"Only be strong and very courageous; be careful to do according to all the law which Moses My servant commanded you; do not turn from it to the right or to the left, so that you may have success wherever you go. "This book of the law shall not depart from your mouth, but you shall meditate on it day and night, so that you may be careful to do according to all that is written in it; for then you will make your way prosperous, and then you will have success. "Have I not commanded you? Be strong and courageous! Do not tremble or be dismayed, for the LORD your God is with you wherever you go."

The instructions and admonitions given in this passage to Joshua are very powerful. The target is clear; and it ignites something in Joshua that motivates him to change the future, not only for himself but for those he was leading.

God already knows the future, but he uses ordinary people like Joshua and you and me to get there. The future is something that can be changed, but it can only happen when we know what we want and how to get there. It is not something that will happen automatically or even easily. It will take hard work and determination to reach the finish line.

As a coach, that is why you are there—to help define the targeted goals that God has for the ones you are helping and then help them make plans to get there and stay on course. In a sense, you will be helping them build their targets.

Think about the targeted goal that the apostle Peter had from God—to preach and teach about Jesus everywhere he went. His mission was clear and precise, and it motivated Peter to unwaveringly put his life on the line when he was brought before the high council to be questioned.

Acts 5:27-29 (NASB)

"When they had brought them, they stood them before the Council. The high priest questioned them, saying, 'We gave you strict orders not to continue teaching in this name, and yet, you have filled Jerusalem with your teaching and intend to bring this man's blood upon us.' But Peter and the apostles answered, 'We must obey God rather than men.'"

When the targeted prize inspires us, and it is something that has God at the center, we will stand against all odds to make it become a reality. This kind of steadfastness is what we must inspire in those we coach.

Paul was one of the first church planters in the Bible. The interesting thing about Paul is that he could have done this task in a lot of different ways. He was highly educated, a powerful leader among the Jews, and religious to a fault. He was the kind of leader you would expect Jesus Christ to choose as one of His disciples; but, as you know, Paul didn't come on the scene as one of the early disciples. Paul's calling experience was much more dramatic than the way the other disciples were called. In fact, the calling that God had for Paul was so big that God had to strike him down from the false religious path that he was on and completely turn him around in another direction. From what we know about Paul, you might expect that God would ask him to focus his energies on interacting with the people he knew, in the areas he knew well, within the customs and traditions that he knew.

However, God had other plans. God gave Paul a target that, when he hit it, the repercussions would touch us today. It was going to be much harder than Paul would ever dream, and there would be many opportunities to turn around and go the other direction and question if it was really a calling from God at all. It would cause him pain, suffering, beatings, shipwrecks, imprisonments, loneliness, and more as he proceeded towards the goal of his calling. Paul knew, however, that it was a target that came from God, so he stayed the course to the end.

Acts 9:5-6 (NASB)

"And he said, 'Who are You, Lord?' And He said, 'I am Jesus whom you are persecuting, but get up and enter the city, and it will be told you what you must do.'"

Paul answered the call, focused on the target, and changed the whole course of his life and future. Paul's future was changed because he was faithful to God's call; and the message that Paul preached has reached us today. He invested his whole life into countless others like you and me. You also can change your future and the futures of those in whom you are investing your life. You can inspire those you are moving from point A to point B to see the targets that God has put before them. You can help others win the prize of achieving their goals.

Deuteronomy 6:5-6 (NASB)

"You shall love the LORD your God with all your heart and with all your soul and with all your might. These words, which I am commanding you today, shall be on your heart."

Matthew 22:37-40 (NASB)

"And He said to him, 'You shall love the Lord your God with all your heart, and with all your soul, and with all your mind. This is the great and foremost commandment. The second is like it, You shall love your neighbor as yourself. On these two commandments depend the whole Law and the Prophets.'"

The point I want to make is that God needs to be at the center of every decision that leads to the targeted goal or prize. God has given each of us a unique purpose and a unique plan; and He equips us with special abilities and spiritual gifts to get the job done.

As you coach, remember that if God isn't at the center of the targeted goal that was set at your first meeting, then the ones you aspire to help will always be frustrated and will never truly be content. Take a moment to make sure that the target of the person you are leading has a God-centered goal attached to it. Here are some powerful questions to ask as you talk about this target:

If you knew that you could not fail, what would you do for the glory of God and the growth of his kingdom?

If God could have his way, how would your life or ministry be different 10 years from now?

What kind of help do you need in clarifying your vision?

What resistance do you expect to the changes you will be making?

How will you handle that resistance? Who can help you in overcoming these obstacles?

Given your current target, what is the best thing that could happen? What is the worst thing that could happen?

….and then ask, "What Else?"

As you meet with the person you are trying to move from point A to point B this month (or bi-weekly), do the following:

1. Spend 10 minutes—Know the Details
2. Spend 10 minutes—Celebrate the Victories
3. Spend 10 minutes—Push through the "Noise" as you discuss current obstacles that may be slowing down this process.
4. Spend 20 minutes—Build the Target
5. Then go to the Worksheet at the end of this chapter.

As your person build his or her target, it is important for them to remember that this must be **their** goal. The reason this book is not called Coaching is because a "coach" is perceived as someone who has all the answers and plans, someone yelling from the sidelines to follow **his** plans precisely. This is not your role.

You are not selling anything, you have no production numbers to reach, there are no tangible rewards, and your success is not based on the achievement of the ones you are helping. You must stay quiet and ask powerful questions before the ones you are coaching can make any progress; this is completely opposite of what we usually perceive a "coach" to be. However, for each powerful question that causes a person to stop in their tracks and think a little deeper, your reward is knowing that you are helping them move from where they are to where they want to be—from point A to point B.

Salesmen sell. They talk about their product and every possible benefit that could come with the use of their product. However, you don't have to sell anything. At the very first meeting, the person you agreed to coach told you exactly what they wanted or where they wanted to be. Then, from the process of you asking them the right questions, they were able to tell YOU exactly how they would get to the target that they had set for themselves. Your job is to keep them moving towards their goals. As you keep track of their targeted goals, you put into motion the type of intermediate actions that move anchors out of people's lives. When anchors are moved, they are then able to really see life changes take place. On the other hand, if you try to sell someone **your** plan for their life, anchors do not get moved. You might see a little action that looks good on the surface, but underneath (on the inside) there is no real change.

However, you can present strategic techniques for a person to work through as a great way to **help** them create a good target. You might try using a graph to show how a large overwhelming task can be broken down into smaller goals.

Here is a hypothetical example:

You ask, "If you knew that you could not fail, what would you do for the glory of God and the growth of His Kingdom?"

Their answer might be, "I don't know. Honestly, I'm so overwhelmed with debt that I can't think about the growth of His Kingdom."

To which you might answer: "Let's take your target of being debt free in five years and put some smaller more specific goals together to get there."

They might say something like, "Ok, well, this one card of $30,000 seems like an overwhelming task."

You might say, "Ok, that is a more specific goal. Now what would you be willing to give to get rid of that debt?"

Then, through thinking about that question, they might answer, "Well, we go out a lot. I suppose if we stop going out to eat, we could put $500 a month towards that card."

To which you answer, "What Else?"

That line is the key for your coaching success. You may end up with five smaller goals from simply asking, "What else?" I suggest that you draw big triangles like the one below to show your person how these goals came from their words, their ideas, and their targets; therefore, they are attainable, and they will be celebrated. As you give them total ownership, they will move anchors to make these things happen.

You can use line graphs, circle graphs, cone graphs, etc., but it all ends up with the same concept. As you build these graphs, along the side make a list of all the possible obstacles that could keep them from achieving this goal. Having all of this on paper will help you as you continue to meet with them, and it will make it easier to make sure that they hit their target.

As you help your person build their Target in the next session, use the following form to a concentrated focus:

Build a Target

What is your target? -

_____

What are 3 smaller steps to reach your target?

1.

_____
_____
_____

2.

_____
_____
_____

3.

_____

_____

_____

Is your target S.M.A.R.T.?

Specific?

_____

Measurable?

_____

Attainable?

_____

Relevant?

_____

Timed?

_____

What will be your reward for achieving
this target?

_____

What will be the consequence for not achieving your target?

_____

What are you willing to give up to reach this target?

_____

What obstacles do you currently need to overcome?

_____

What goals can we celebrate a victory with so far?

_____

How did you reward yourself when you achieved those smaller goals?

_____

Who is in your life right now that can help you with your next step?

1.

_____

2.

_____

3.

_____

How is God at the center of your target?

_____

How can God be more of your target?

_____

Psalms 138:8 (NASB)

"The LORD will accomplish what concerns me; Your lovingkindness, O LORD, is everlasting; Do not forsake the works of Your hands."

Ephesians 6:10-13 (NASB)

"Finally, be strong in the Lord and in the strength of His might. Put on the full armor of God, so that you will be able to stand firm against the schemes of the devil. For our struggle is not against flesh and blood, but against the rulers, against the powers, against the world forces of this darkness, against the spiritual forces of wickedness in the heavenly places. Therefore, take up the full armor of God, so that you will be able to resist in the evil day, and having done everything, to stand firm."

Read the rest of Ephesians 6 and make sure that you have the full armor of God on as you continue to move towards your target. Without understanding the battle ahead, you will not be able to change the future.

Chapter 5

Assess the Resources

You have so many more resources than
just those you read about in the Bible.
First and foremost, you have a complete
Bible of 66 books at your fingertips; and
you can consult and openly read it any
time you want. I hope this will always
be true. Secondly, you have more
books written about the topics contained
in the Bible than you could read in five
lifetimes, which almost makes me
hesitate to write another one! Thirdly,
most of us (whether we know it or not)
are surrounded by people who can help
us in our Christian walk.

Therefore, in your endeavor to "grow
grass on rocks," it is your responsibility
to remind the people you coach that
they are not alone as you continue to
move them from point A to point B. You
have abundant resources, not only for

yourself but for those you coach, all around you; and you need to take the time to assess those resources that are available to those you are helping move towards their targets. The right resources used at the right moments will increase, not only your odds for success in this endeavor, but for the one's you coach, as well.

When we talk about resources, the world almost always thinks about money and the things that money can buy. Indeed, it is hard not to be distracted by what the world considers wealth. In addition, the world also considers natural abilities, physical attractiveness, personality, talents, and charm when measuring a person's likelihood of achieving success in this world.

However, none of these things are what God looks at when he measures your worth. In fact, sometimes these are the very things that can distract us from the resources that God wants us to recognize and use. God can and often does take the insignificant and foolish things of this world and uses them for

His glory; and you should never limit yourself or anyone else to the standards of this world when God has given you so much more.

Solomon of the Bible was one of the wealthiest men who ever lived. He had everything he could ever want at his fingertips, including physical strength; yet he wrote, "Vanity of vanities, says the Preacher, all is vanity!" (Ecclesiastes 12:8 NASB) Indeed, Solomon is just one of many in the Bible who knew and understood that wealth and position is not everything and that there is so much more to be desired; and I want to use Nehemiah, another notable character in the Bible, as a case study for the remainder of this chapter.

The book of Nehemiah gives us a guideline on how to build upon our resources when pursuing a target goal. Nehemiah was the cupbearer to the Persian King Artaxerxes during his 41-year reign, and Nehemiah enjoyed a life of luxury and ease inside the palace. However, there came a time when Nehemiah heard about the broken-down walls around his beloved city of Jerusalem, and he felt compelled to do something about it. God put it in his heart to leave the palace and help his people in Israel by supervising the construction of a protective wall around the city of Jerusalem. Thus, Nehemiah was a leader who had to move people from point A to point B by doing something that may have seemed impossible. He had to "grow grass on rocks."

Nehemiah 1:4 (NIV)

"When I heard these things, I sat down and wept. For some days I mourned and fasted and prayed before the God of heaven."

When Nehemiah first heard about the problem, he felt an overwhelming sense of sorrow at the situation; and his first recourse was to give it up to God through prayer and fasting. Notice that Nehemiah did not sit down and try to figure out what **he** could do to fix the situation in his own power. Instead, He knew that God was his best Resource;

and that is where he went first. Obviously, Nehemiah had power and money on his side; yet he spent "some days" on his knees before God!

Nehemiah 1:5-7 (NIV)

"Then I said, 'O Lord, God of heaven, the great and awesome God, who keeps his covenant of love with those who love him and obey his commands, 6 let your ear be attentive and your eyes open to hear the prayer your servant is praying before you day and night for your servants, the people of Israel. I confess the sins we Israelites, including myself and my father's house, have committed against you. 7 We have acted very wickedly toward you. We have not obeyed the commands, decrees, and laws you gave your servant Moses.'"

In this passage, Nehemiah already had a personal relationship with God. This fact begs for us to re-evaluate our own personal relationship with God and to take inventory of the resources we usually turn to. When you have a problem, where do you most often turn?

Sadly, the answer is that most people go to their phones or computers to google their problems in hopes of finding a quick solution. However, I hope that Nehemiah will cause you to rethink your ideas about resources and make your relationship with God your priority, and thus your first resource.

When Nehemiah hears about the situation and assesses the magnitude of the target ahead, he knows that his best resource is to turn to God in prayer and call out to Him. He also knows that God is not impressed with arrogance or worldly position, and he addresses Almighty God in humility and with a servant's attitude. In addition, Nehemiah uses his knowledge of God's Word (which is another powerful resource that we all have) and applies it to the situation. He believes in the power of God and the power of His Word and calls on both as he moves forward towards getting the walls rebuilt.

Nehemiah 2:5 (NIV)

"And I answered the king, "If it pleases the king and if your servant has found favor in his sight, let him send me to the city in Judah where my fathers are buried so that I can rebuild it."

As Nehemiah was weeping and calling upon God, the king noticed and asked him what was causing such distress. Nehemiah realized that it was now time to tap into his natural resources. For him to do what God wanted him to do, Nehemiah knew he would have to be released from his current responsibility as cupbearer to the king.

You, too, will find that there may be some situations in your life that require that you prioritize their importance in the long run. In doing so, you may have to face an employer or other person in authority and let them know that you have something else that you must do, and it may take your focus away from your current position(s). For example, you might have to turn down a second job or committee position to free up your time to do what God wants you to do. Time is a valuable resource, but it must be used wisely.

In the world we live in, people are literally bombarded with appointments and obligations of every description. Most jobs, for example, have multiple extra-curricular jobs and committees that can take up every waking moment of a person's life. In addition, parents often feel guilty if their children aren't involved in every available sport or activity; and many of these activities are run by parent volunteers. These are the types of situations that call for you to prioritize your time and free it up to cultivate your relationship with God, as well as for time to do what He is asking you to do in His Kingdom. When you realize (or someone you are coaching realizes) that time is the biggest hurdle in reaching a goal, that is when you or they must be bold and face up against any force that takes them away from reaching their goal.

In our case study, it is evident that Nehemiah highly respected the authority of the king and appreciated his position as cupbearer in the palace; and his approach in asking the king's permission to go to Judah is done in a spirit of respect and humility. By humbly explaining his cause, Nehemiah takes personal ownership of his target goal. He obviously does not use the excuse that he can't go forward because of his current position or responsibilities.

Instead of using the obvious obstacles and distractions in his life to keep him from his goal, Nehemiah takes the necessary steps to remove those obstacles. In essence, he clears his calendar to do God's work at hand; and this is what you may have to do, also, if you want to be successful in reaching your goal.

Nehemiah 2:11-12 (NIV)

"I went to Jerusalem, and after staying there three days I set out during the night with a few men. I had not told anyone what my God had put in my heart to do for Jerusalem. There were

no mounts with me except the one I was riding on."

As Nehemiah moves forward, he understands the obstacles and the enemies that would try to keep him from his target of rebuilding the walls. Therefore, he constructs a series of small goals that will lead him to the ultimate target. In chapter three, he sets out with the smaller goal of selecting a few good men who would help him reach his target; and he begins this task by assessing the resources available in the different men. By learning their names and the gifts and talents that they possessed, Nehemiah was able to determine where he could use them in the building of the wall. Thus, by taking one step at a time towards the goal, the big task ahead was not so daunting.

Nehemiah had a very ambitious goal ahead. Therefore, he needed many people to help him in that endeavor; and his job was to give each group of men a set of clear objectives with personalized tasks based on their abilities and gifts. You and the ones you coach, on the other hand, may not require a lot of people to reach your goals. However, never underestimate the resources that you will find in people. Sometimes, a single person may have the exact answer that you need to reach a smaller goal; and that one answer may be a huge steppingstone to your ultimate goal.

On the other hand, people can be your main source of failure, as well. You will often encounter negative people who only want to sabotage your success; and those kinds of negative resources also must be assessed on whether they are helping or hurting your progress.

In Nehemiah Chapter 3, for example, we learn that Nehemiah had some negative men called Tekoites who refused to work on the wall. Instead of being helpful in reaching his goal, they started weighing him down and slowing down his progress. Eventually, in Chapter 4, we see how their outright opposition to Nehemiah's cause drove him back again to calling on God, his first resource.

Nehemiah 4:4-5 (NIV)

"Hear us, O our God, for we are despised. Turn their insults back on their own heads. Give them over as plunder in a land of captivity. 5 Do not cover up their guilt or blot out their sins from your sight, for they have thrown insults in the face of the builders."

Once again, Nehemiah goes to his first Resource, and asks for help. Faced with insults and threats against his targeted goal, he prays to God and prepares for the enemy's attack. Knowing that the attack is inevitable, he trusts God and keeps working towards his goal. In addition, he prepares the people for the obstacles that are coming and gets them ready to take on the upcoming challenges.

Nehemiah 4:13-14 (NIV)

"Therefore I stationed some of the people behind the lowest points of the wall at the exposed places, posting

them by families, with their swords, spears and bows. 14 After I looked things over, I stood up and said to the nobles, the officials and the rest of the people, "Don't be afraid of them. Remember the Lord, who is great and awesome, and fight for your brothers, your sons and your daughters, your wives and your homes."

This wasn't an easy road for Nehemiah, and he had to constantly be in prayer. He used Godly conviction and wisdom through each problem that emerged and reminded those he was with that God is bigger than any enemy or struggle. He also lets the people know that there would be consequences for failure to do the right thing if they gave in to the enemy. While giving all the praise and glory to God, Nehemiah convinces those around him to choose to do the right thing over the easy thing and keeps the people from giving up or running away from the target that God has given him.

Nehemiah 5:9 (NIV)

"So I continued, 'What you are doing is not right. Shouldn't you walk in the fear of our God to avoid the reproach of our Gentile enemies?'"

Finally, in Chapter 6, we see Nehemiah pushing through to the finish line as he presses toward his God-given target. However, the enemy continues to try and stop him in every possible way. He endures rumors and even blackmail against his character and his motivation for building the wall; but he never fails to vindicate himself before the people and continuously goes to God for strength and help. He doesn't fall into many of the traps of life that people normally succumb to because he faithfully prays and trusts in God while knowing and obeying His Word.

Nehemiah 6:13-16 (NIV)

"He had been hired to intimidate me so that I would commit a sin by doing this, and then they would give me a bad name to discredit me...So the wall was

completed on the twenty-fifth of Elul, in fifty-two days. When all our enemies heard about this, all the surrounding nations were afraid and lost their self-confidence, because they realized that this work had been done with the help of our God."

Nehemiah understood that the target was to rebuild the wall, but he also understood that the actual building of the wall would not be the challenge. The real challenge would come through the day-to-day small obstacles and trials that would have to be overcome along the way. Therefore, Nehemiah wisely assessed each of his resources and used each one to reach his goal; and, in so doing, he managed to win the hearts of the people.

In the Bible, we don't often see committees taking on huge challenges. Instead, we see God calling individual men and women to step up to the plate and answer His call. If you are working towards a God-sized plan, then God will give you the means and the resources to accomplish it. Resources come in a variety of ways—people, money, time, churches, programs, books, and most importantly in God and His Word.

As you meet with the person you are trying to move from point A to point B this month (or bi-weekly), do the following:

1. Spend 10 minutes—Know the Details
2. Spend 10 minutes—Celebrate the Victories
3. Spend 10 minutes—Push through the "Noise" as you discuss current obstacles that are slowing down the process.
4. Spend 10 minutes—Build the Target by reminding them that this was the target that they set.
5. Spend 15 minutes—Assess the Resources they have all around them.
6. Then go to the Worksheet at the end of this chapter.

It is important to help people discover the many resources that are available to them as you move them from point A to point B. You can begin by asking some powerful questions that will help them not only to see the obvious resources but also will open a whole new world of possibilities. If the brainstorming begins to slow down, you can move the conversation to questions on how to find more resources in their life. Remember, an idea will be far stronger and move anchors more easily when the idea comes from the one you are coaching rather than from you.

Try using the Resource Mapping exercise located at the end of this chapter to discover all the resources available with the person you are coaching. The chances are good that they will be surprised by how many resources they have available to them daily.

Building the Resources

What are some of the current resources you are using to reach your target?

_____

_____

_____

_____

_____

What are some other resources that
would help in reaching your target?
Brainstorm! What else?

_____

_____

_____

_____

_____

What changes can you make to utilize
your existing resources more
effectively?

_____

_____

_____

_____

_____

What steps can you take to discover
new resources?

_____

_____

_____

_____

_____

Who do you know that has gone through a similar experience?

_____

_____

_____

Resource Mapping

Using post-it notes and a large sheet of paper on a wall – write each idea on a post it note and put it on the wall.

Step 1: Write the Target across the top.

Step 2: Write 5 smaller goals that will help you reach the targeted goal underneath the target.

Step 3: Brainstorm all the resources in your life and place them on post-it notes all over the wall.

Step 4: Brainstorm all the resources you need in your life and place them on the wall.

Step 5: Organize the post-it notes into each goal they would work best for.

Step 6: Write down a plan of attack for each goal using the resources underneath on the post-it notes.

Step 7: Write down a timeline for each goal.

Step 8: Write down who or what will keep you accountable for each goal.

Step 9: Write down the reward you will give yourself when you accomplish each goal.

If you're still struggling, you can try a Google search for the latest brainstorming techniques:

- http://www.mindtools.com/brainst m.html
- http://personalexcellence.co/blog/2 5-brainstorming-techniques/
- http://designshack.net/articles/insp iration/10-tips-for-effective-creative-brainstorming

(No affiliation with these websites, just the top 3 that popped up on Google at the time of this writing)

...

Chapter 6

Identify the Obstacles

It is important to see the big picture and know exactly what the target is as you move forward with someone from point A to point B. If you take your eyes off the big picture, the mundane day-to-day living can overtake you. You must identify the obstacles in a person's life that have the potential to distract them from their goals. Another way to approach this aspect of "growing grass on rocks" is to have the person you are meeting with tell you how things are going for them and what progress they think is being made towards their goal. You might start with asking them this question:

What are three ways you moved closer to your goal since we last met? ...and then ask, "What Else?"

In the answer to this question, you may observe how the focus on an obstacle has taken the place of the main target. Think of it like an auto assembly line. If you ask the person who assembles the interior carpet, "How's it going?" they may say, "Well, we have shaved three seconds off the installation time" or "The latest configuration of chairs makes it impossible to install the carpet correctly." Whatever they might say about the details of carpet installation tells you where their head is – which would be on that very small part of the auto assembly line.

Focusing on the intricate details in the assembly of an automobile is probably fine to most people, especially to those who are hiring in those areas; but for what we are talking about, these are all bad answers. In the car assembly analogy, the person who is focusing on the finished product would want to hear something about the total production of cars. He would want to hear answers like, "This last month we produced 25% more cars as a company!" or "The total sales of cars in our factory have gone up by 10%!" He might also hear something in a negative vein, as well, such as "The morale of the company has dropped because of the lack of new car designs." In either case, the answer focuses on the big picture of the targeted goal.

The point is that we want to look for people who can keep their eyes on the big picture, the larger target, the important goals—people who do not become bogged down and distracted by the obstacles that come every day. It is much like the bricklayer who sees himself as someone who is just laying brick rather than building fantastic buildings, or the road worker who is just pouring pavement instead of seeing himself as a key part of moving people across the world. It might be a stretch to compare all these examples to how people see themselves in their personal situations, but we want to help them quickly identify the obstacles that have the potential to keep them from reaching their goals.

Keep their eyes on the ultimate prize!

Most people see themselves within a system over which they have little or no control, and they can't see the big picture of what they can be. Instead, they resort to just doing their job, putting in their time, and somehow coping with the forces outside of their control. Life is so much more than this, and God has created within us unique attributes and purposes that will accomplish far greater things than we can imagine—if we look past the setbacks and discouragements of today.

Ephesians 3:20-21 (NASB)

"Now to Him who is able to do far more abundantly beyond all that we ask or think, according to the power that works within us, to Him be the glory in the church and in Christ Jesus to all generations forever and ever. Amen."

How many counselors, pastors, social workers, friends, and family have heard those they care about or counsel with talk about all the outside influences that keep them from where they think they should be. As coaches, we cannot let the people we are working with fall into this classic trap. We must get across the point that others do not define us and that there is nothing we can't do if we take the time to identify the obstacles and work through the steps it takes to overcome them.

Philippians 4:12-13 (NASB)

"I know how to get along with humble means, and I also know how to live in

prosperity; in any and every circumstance I have learned the secret of being filled and going hungry, both of having abundance and suffering need. I can do all things through Him who strengthens me."

My children come to me often complaining about their brother or sister. It can be about a myriad of things, but it is always about what the other one did to them or took away from them or even said to them that is ruining their day. This is a common situation that parents and teachers must deal with daily. As a parent, I usually talk to the other child who then proceeds to explain through tears or anger about how the other one did something to them first. On and on this "blame game" goes until I finally say, "Ok, play time is over, it's time to clean your room!" or "Get ready for bed," depending on the time of day. Suddenly, our kids realize that they have forfeited the fun they could have had all for the sake of revenge or vindication. Because they took their eyes off what they really wanted and focused on the immediate offense instead, they now must live with what they did not want. Of course, with children there are times when parent intervention is needed, but nine times out of ten it is something that can easily be solved without losing the joy of the moment.

We can understand this analogy with children because we see it all the time, and because children lack the maturity to see past the moment. In addition, such behavior is expected of children. However, the problem is that many adults have not outgrown their childish behavior. They are all too willing to give up the greater goals in life because they can't get past the obstacles of today. Therefore, as coaches, we need to help them identify those obstacles that keep them from reaching their goals.

Individuals are not the only ones who get bogged down in events of the past and find it difficult to move on towards their goals. Companies and organizations suffer with the same dilemma. Most of the conversations that take place in company meetings are overwhelmingly about either past performances or mistakes or about the fear of what is happening in the future: last month's sales, new budget stipulations, last quarter's earnings, promotions or firings, products released by competitors, what other companies are doing, and on and one.

In companies and organizations, some of this kind of talk may be warranted; but when our personal conversations are dominated with the past, we tend to speak in reactive or defensive tones and actions. Consequently, we jump to temporary solutions to stabilize the current state of affairs. Instead of focusing on our goals, our targets, and our road to success, we completely forget what we set out to do in the first place.

Jumping to temporary solutions can be devastating for companies and organizations, especially when they wake up one day and realize that they have moved so far from the path they had started that they aren't sure why they exist. In the church world, for example, I have seen churches announce new programs and events that have so little of God in them or Bible principles in them that if you didn't see the word "church" in their name, you would just assume it was a new kind of club. Obviously, they have forgotten their reason for existing.

The same kind of thing can easily happen when we try to help people reach their goals. That is why it is very necessary to have clearly defined missions and core values, not only for companies and organizations, but for individuals as well. When goals are clearly defined, they will not get lost in the setbacks and problems of everyday living.

As you coach people from point A to point B, there will undoubtedly be some meetings that will be dominated by the obstacles that are presently keeping them from their goals. Those times together can become a sad state of "woe is me" instead of joyfully celebrating all that God has done in their lives as they have moved on towards their main target. Therefore, you must help keep people focused on their goals by identifying the obstacles and brainstorming how they can move past them.

As you meet with the person you are trying to move from point A to point B this month (or bi-weekly), do the following:

1. Spend 5 minutes—Know the Details
2. Spend 5 minutes—Celebrate the Victories
3. Spend 10 minutes—Push through the "Noise" as you discuss current obstacles.
4. Spend 10 minutes—Build the Target by reminding them that this was a target that they set.
5. Spend 10 minutes—Assess the Resources they have available to them.
6. Spend 15 minutes—Identify the Obstacles to keep their eyes on the prize.
7. Then go to the Worksheet at the end of this chapter.

Remember the parable of the "boiled frog". If you place a frog in a pot of boiling water, it will immediately try to scramble out; but if you place the frog in room-temperature water and don't scare him, he'll stay put. Now, if the pot sits on a heat source and you gradually turn up the temperature, something very interesting happens. As the temperature rises from 70 to 80 degrees F., the frog will do nothing. In fact, he will show every sign of enjoying himself. However, as the temperature gradually increases, the frog will become groggier and groggier, until he is unable to climb out of the pot. Though there is nothing restraining him, the frog will sit there and boil. Why? Because the frog's internal apparatus for sensing threats to his survival is geared towards the sudden changes in his environment—not to slow, gradual changes.

We have seen this same phenomenon happen in all facets of our American society, including the life of many churches; and you will also see it happening in the individual people you are trying to move from point A to point B. It is called "growing grass on rocks" because we get used to things in life just being the way they are. People will even use the excuse of "That's just the way I am" or "That's just the way it is" when they don't realize how they have slowly let their excuses (obstacles) weigh them down and keep them from achieving their goals.

Let's step back and see how Paul was able to make the following statement:

Philippians 4:12-13 (NASB)

"I know how to get along with humble means, and I also know how to live in prosperity; in any and every circumstance I have learned the secret of being filled and going hungry, both of having abundance and suffering need. I can do all things through Him who strengthens me."

Paul was a human being just like you and me, so how was he able to say these things to the Philippian people? What brought him to such a conclusion? Perhaps it was because he was able to clearly identify the obstacles and saw them for what they were.

Philippians 3:2-3 (NASB)

"Beware of the dogs, beware of the evil workers, beware of the false circumcision; for we are the true circumcision, who worship in the Spirit of God and glory in Christ Jesus and put no confidence in the flesh,"

There are going to be those in this world who have evil on their minds and will try to put their evil intentions on you. There will also be those in life who tell you what they think you must do but who don't really know the truth. If you know the truth of Christ Jesus, then no one can define who you are or what you are supposed to be. Don't put too much confidence in your own flesh either or in what you can accomplish in your flesh because you have something more powerful than your fleshly abilities—the

Holy Spirit dwelling inside you. In this verse above, Paul clearly identified the real obstacles that we face, and he boldly spoke the truth of why they are wrong and how to move past them.

In the next verses, Paul reveals that he has faced distractions and obstacles and how he overcame them for the sake of gaining Christ in his life, which was his life goal. He declares his complete dedication to his goal by saying that what he stands to gain is far greater that the things he has given up in his quest to know Christ.

Philippians 3:7-8 (NASB)

"But whatever things were gain to me, those things I have counted as loss for the sake of Christ. More than that, I count all things to be loss in view of the surpassing value of knowing Christ Jesus my Lord, for whom I have suffered the loss of all things, and count

them but rubbish so that I may gain Christ,"

Paul does not pretend that the obstacles he has faced are not real, nor does he give himself credit for overcoming them. Even while acknowledging his own struggles with the things, he has endured, he bravely points them toward what is more important and the goals that are ahead:

Philippians 3:12-13 (NASB)

"Not that I have already obtained it or have already become perfect, but I press on so that I may lay hold of that for which also I was laid hold of by Christ Jesus. Brethren, I do not regard myself as having laid hold of it yet; but one thing I do: forgetting what lies behind and reaching forward to what lies ahead,"

Paul presses continually toward what lies ahead for him; but at the same time, he also encourages others who need to move from where they are to where they want or need to be to fulfill their God-given dreams, as well. He says, "I press on toward the goal for the prize of the upward call of God in Christ Jesus." (Phil. 3:14, NASB) Thus, while humbly sharing his own experiences, he motivates the people around him to also identify the obstacles that they will face as they, too, press toward their goals. He reminds them of the great victory ahead when they will win the prize that has been set before them.

Philippians 3:20-21 (NASB)

"For our citizenship is in heaven, from which also we eagerly wait for a Savior, the Lord Jesus Christ; who will transform the body of our humble state into conformity with the body of His glory, by the exertion of the power that

He has even 'to subject all things to Himself."

Once again, Paul reminds them of the greater target. As a leader, you also must constantly remind the ones you coach of the target goals that they have set—the target that was identified by them and set by them with a clear path in how they would get there. You are the catalyst that should continue to put this target before them so that they won't allow anything to distract them from the victory that they want to experience. It should not be a surprise to you when obstacles get in the way of the person you are meeting with. Distractions and setbacks are common to everyone, but it is your job to keep them focused on the greater good. Paul can identify the obstacles in the lives of the Philippians and to refocus them on the greater goals; and although you don't see the actual refocusing process, you can read the admonitions he gives them for success:

Philippians 4:4-7 (NASB)

"Rejoice in the Lord always; again I will say, rejoice! Let your gentle spirit be known to all men. The Lord is near. Be anxious for nothing, but in everything by prayer and supplication with thanksgiving let your requests be made known to God. And the peace of God, which surpasses all comprehension, will guard your hearts and your minds in Christ Jesus."

As you can see, he gives them a clear formula of how to get their focus back on the things that truly matter.

Philippians 4:8-9 (NASB)

"Finally, brethren, whatever is true, whatever is honorable, whatever is right, whatever is pure, whatever is lovely, whatever is of good repute, if there is

any excellence and if anything worthy of praise, dwell on these things. The things you have learned and received and heard and seen in me, practice these things, and the God of peace will be with you."

If they will practice these things that Paul has humbly admonished them to do, then they will experience the confidence to say with Paul, "I can do all things through Him who strengthens me!" (Phil. 4:13, NASB) Nothing will be impossible for them, and nothing will be impossible for you or the people you meet with monthly.

A few years ago, my wife bought me a puzzle of Disneyland. I love Disneyland and have been there many times. This is an understatement because I have been there so many times that I could describe in detail every inch of the park, both inside the park and in the backstage as well. As I dumped the thousand-plus-piece puzzle on my desk to begin putting it all together, I realized that it was still going to be a challenge. Having a clear picture of what it was supposed to look like didn't take away the challenge of fitting each individual piece together; and it took many hours to get even a small section of the puzzle to come together. However, the fact that I had the big picture of the park in my mind made it easier to fit the smaller sections together. Slowly but surely, I worked on one section of the park at a time—Tomorrow Land here, Adventure Land over there, Frontier Land back there. As I meticulously placed each section of land into its proper place in the park, the big picture slowly started to emerge. Keeping my mind on the larger target—the big picture—helped me put together the smaller details as each Land came together.

It's a lot the same with us as we strive to reach our goals in life; and knowing this principle will help you coach other people to do the same. You must remind people of the big picture, the target that they want to hit or the goal they want to reach, when they come up against the obstacles that threaten their success. As you outline the steps, they need to take to get past each obstacle, you must show them how each step they take forward will be like fitting a small piece of the puzzle together to make their dream come true. In doing so, the big picture of their desired goal will slowly emerge.

Identifying the Obstacles:

What is the current obstacle you are facing?

_____

What would be a victory over this obstacle?

_____

What resources do you have to help overcome this obstacle?

_____

What resources do you need to obtain to help overcome this obstacle?

_____

How can you gain the resources needed?

_____

What are some "Out of the Box" ways you could overcome this obstacle?

_____

_____

_____

What are the next 3 actions you need to take to overcome this obstacle?

1.

_____

_____

_____

_____

2.

_____

_____

_____

_____

3.

_____

_____

_____

_____

How will you celebrate victory over this obstacle?

_____

What is your timeframe to accomplish each action above and complete each action above?

_____

How will overcoming this obstacle move you closer to your desired goal and target?

_____

Chapter 7

Shoot the Arrows!

By this time, you have interacted with the person you are trying to move from point A to point B for several months. Not only have you become familiar with their hopes and dreams, but you have built a strong enough relationship with them that you should be able to ask the tough questions and move them towards their goals. You have spent time celebrating the victories in their life and helped them to push past the various distractions and noises so that they can focus on what is truly important. You have helped them to define a clear target goal that they want to reach and then helped them to identify the obstacles that could prevent them from reaching that goal. Together, you have assessed the resources in their life that they can use to overcome those obstacles; and now it is time to shoot the arrows at the target!

One of the greatest myths in life is that we are somehow entitled to a great life. We have entitlement issues because of what we see others have, and we just assume that life will be fair. Why is that? Where is the Life Handbook that says, "All things start equally; and somehow, somewhere, or through someone, you will get all the things you need to achieve happiness, success, or possessions"? Here is the most important lesson that I believe you could ever teach someone as you attempt to "grow grass on rocks": *Life is not fair, and you are ultimately responsible for what happens in your life!*

I'm sure that you can point to many people in your life who have been given far more chances, breaks, tools, money, promotions, or opportunities in life than they deserved. Then, on the other hand, some of them may have deserved some of those things, but you may wonder why they should be so successful when you've not been given the same advantages?

At the other end of the spectrum, you can also point to many people around the world who just don't seem to have a chance. It is not fair that some grow up in abusive homes, or some are forced to live in poverty, while others are victims of racism, as well as many other examples of disadvantage. It is not fair that some are handed family businesses or inherit great sums of money that they did not work for while others are victims of their parent's crimes. It's not fair that a drunk driver hit your car, the tornado hit your town, or the stock market crashed just when you invested your money.

Your list of unfair things that have happened in your life can go on and on, and you can continue to list all the ways that the world comes against you and puts you in situations that many others do not have to face. In the end, however, what will that list mean to the world? It will mean Nothing! Regardless of your situation, the fact is that you are ultimately responsible for what happens in your life, and no one really cares about your sad story. That may sound harsh, so let's ask why that is? The reason that no one really cares about your sad story is because everyone has their own sad story to talk about if they want to. While you are telling them about your sad story, they may be thinking, "If you only knew about me and my life, you would not think your story is so bad."

Everyone in this world, whether they are rich or poor, successful, or not, famous or nobody—EVERYONE carries some kind of heavy load, but the difference in how they are perceived by others is in how they have adjusted and moved on with their lives. So, as a leader, you must somehow encourage the ones you coach to get over their excuses and sad stories, regardless of how legitimate they may be, and shoot the arrows towards the target goals they have set. The message you want to internalize, not only for yourself but for those you coach, as well, is to take control of your life and never let another person or thing define the success that you will have in life.

The reality of life is that we should only complain about things that we have the ability to change. When a plane tragically falls from the sky, our first response is not, "I hate gravity! It always causes us so much pain!" No, we understand that gravity is something that we have no control over. Instead, when a plane crashes, the focus normally centers around things like pilot error, mechanical failure, bad weather, or bad coordinates from the tower. These are the things that could have been prevented, and these are the possible reasons that people died—not gravity. The point I want to make is that all the things we usually complain about in life—our weight, not enough time, our jobs, our families, our marriages, not enough money, and so on—are all things that we do have a lot of control over. Make sure you really understand that point. The fact is that we spend very little time complaining about things we have no control over; but ironically, the things that we **are** complaining about are the very things that we can change in our life!

You are the one who makes poor diet choices.

You are the one who chooses to stay late in the office or stay up all night.

You are the one who chooses the long-distant relationship.

You are the one who chooses not to go to your kids' activities.

You are the one who allows people to talk to you in a derogatory way.

You are the one who doesn't help clean up the house.

You are the one buying the toys.

You are the one who chooses to work on Sunday mornings.

You are the one who avoids getting to know new people.

Insert your own target here and understand that no one is keeping you from reaching your goals but you.

Obviously, there are some things that may have happened to you as you grew up that didn't happen to others; but there are things that others have experienced that did not happen to you, as well. Some people must overcome the worst home environments that you can imagine or the worst tragedies that you could possibly imagine. However, for every one of those life-debilitating experiences, I can show you historic examples of people who didn't let the tragedies of their lives define who they were. Many people in the past who didn't appear to have a chance, have risen above their tragedies and achieved greatness. The fact is that we choose how the experiences of life will affect our futures; and, conversely, we choose when something is going to keep us from hitting our target.

This chapter is about "shooting the arrows" of determination, motivation, and application, as well as the "arrows" that God has given you through your spiritual gifts, to claim victory in your life; and you want your arrows to hit the target. Whatever your dream or desire, you must understand that no one can keep you from reaching your goals but YOU.

Abraham Lincoln rose from the ashes of poverty and lack of opportunity to become one of our greatest presidents. George Washington Carver, who was born into slavery but became a famous American botanist and inventor, had a great quote in which he said, "Ninety-nine percent of all failures come from people who have a habit of making excuses." Joni Eareckson Tada, the CEO of Joni and Friends International Disability Center, became a quadriplegic in a wheelchair after a diving accident that left her paralyzed from her neck down with not even the use of her hands at the age of 17. Nevertheless, after two years of intensive rehabilitation, she went on to write over 50 books and paint high-detailed fine art paintings by holding special pencils and brushes with her teeth. The things she has accomplished are too many to mention here but serve to prove that excuses do not exist for those who have the will to succeed. Inspiration is a key element in getting anything accomplished, and to "shoot an arrow" successfully towards the target, a person must get his or her emotions involved. All the talking, planning, and dreaming about reaching a goal must culminate in hitting the target; otherwise, it just remains a fantasy. Hitting the target is when all the excuses are exposed for what they are—LIES—and the victory is won!

On a weekly basis I stand at the church door on Sunday mornings and say goodbye to as many people as I can as they leave the church. As a pastor, I have always been intrigued and perplexed by the variety of parting remarks that I hear every week. Most people will tell me how great the service was; and although I do not need to hear this because I don't do church work to get accolades from people, it is still nice to hear that someone was really moved by the worship or by a word in the service. Sometimes a family will spend a good amount of time telling me how they loved worshipping together or how a testimony spoken was exactly what they have been wrestling with and how they are going to be making some dramatic changes in their life.

However, the ironic thing that inevitably happens week after week is that the very next person to shake my hand will tell me about three things that were unacceptable about the service. On the one hand, one person will speak of how his life was changed by the music, for example, and on the other hand, the next person will say something like how she couldn't even think because of the music. Both people attended the same service, but their responses were very different. Why is that?

I have concluded that it is not the service at all, nor is it some kind of different experience based on where the person was sitting. The only logical explanation is in the eyes, ears, and minds of the people attending the service. One chooses to see all the positive things that can be a blessing in their life, and the other chooses to see all the negative things that can distract them in their life. Thus, we choose our responses in life.

The millions of people who move from church to church from week to week in search of the perfect place that will meet their needs testify to the fact that everyone has a choice in how they experience life. As you focus on the target ahead and the intermediate goals to get there, it will be up to you to decide if you will shoot the arrows and claim the victory. Most of the time just "shooting the arrow" is half the battle. Once the arrow is in the air, the rest of the battle will take care of itself. However, if you never shoot the arrow, you will continue to have the results you have always had. There is a saying that says, "Insanity is doing the same thing you have always done but expecting different results". Something must change, so just "shoot the arrow!"

In the Bible, Paul traveled from city to city as one of the first church planters. During his travels, he wrote letters to the different churches that he had planted in order to keep them encouraged or to answer the questions that arose from new church members. One of these fascinating letters was written to the Thessalonians. As I read these letters, I see a pastor admonishing his congregation to stay focused on the target that is before them and to not be afraid to shoot the arrows. In the following passage, the "arrow" that Paul wants his congregation to shoot is the arrow of the power of the Holy Spirit.

1 Thessalonians 1:5-6 (NASB)

"For our gospel did not come to you in word only, but also in power and in the Holy Spirit and with full conviction; just

as you know what kind of men we proved to be among you for your sake. You also became imitators of us and of the Lord, having received the word in much tribulation with the joy of the Holy Spirit,"

The hard questions you may have to ask the person you are coaching are these: "Are you just talk with no action? Do you merely like to talk and dream about all the great ideas God has given you to know and do in this world? Or will you shoot the arrow of belief in the power of the Holy Spirit within you and become an imitator of those who have gone before you, including our Lord?" The bottom line is that we can talk about all the obstacles, the resources we have, the distractions and problems involved, and the strategies we will use; but until we start shooting the arrows, we will just be full of empty words. At some point as you move people from where they are to where they need to be, you will have to strongly encourage them to try to shoot for the goal. Their first attempt may be a complete failure, but their attempt must be so bold that no one will doubt their intention.

When the Thessalonians shot their arrow of faith, Paul reported that people heard about it all the way to Macedonia and Achaia and "every place your faith toward God has gone forth." (1 Thessalonians 1:8 NASB) That basically meant that their bold faith was so powerful that it had an impact everywhere they went and upon everyone they told.

The truth is that you don't have to be an amazing orator or live a perfect life to motivate people to achieve their goals. People will imitate you if you have the power of the Holy Spirit leading you as you "grow grass on rocks". God has used many unschooled, ordinary men to spread His Word all around the world. Yet, Paul was an educated man with lots of leadership capabilities, and even he wrote about how he was successful **only** through the power of the Holy Spirit.

1 Thessalonians 2:4-7 (NASB)

"But just as we have been approved by God to be entrusted with the gospel, so we speak, not as pleasing men, but God who examines our hearts. For we never came with flattering speech, as you know, nor with a pretext for greed – God is witness – nor did we seek glory from men, either from you or from others, even through apostles of Christ we might have asserted our authority. But we proved to be gentle among you, as a nursing mother tenderly cares for her own children."

You have been given an incredible opportunity to help move someone from point A to point B; and I ask you to not take that task lightly. If you have begun this process, God has chosen you for a very special role in life—a role that, in Biblical examples, He only entrusted to those whose hearts He had examined. Today, just as it was in Biblical times, God is not looking for talent or special abilities to be the element of change in people's lives. Rather, He is looking for those whose hearts are pure and who demonstrate the fruit of the Holy Spirit, such as gentleness and love, in their lives. These are the ones through which the Holy Spirit can do His work.

As you meet with the person you are trying to move from point A to point B this month (or bi-weekly), do the following:

1. Spend 5 minutes—Know the Details
2. Spend 5 minutes—Celebrate the Victories
3. Spend 10 minutes—Push through the "noise" as you discuss current obstacles.

4. Spend 10 minutes—Build the Target by reminding them that this was the target they set.
5. Spend 10 minutes—Assess the Resources available to them.
6. Spend 10 minutes—Identify the Obstacles
7. Then go to the Worksheet at the end of this chapter.

If you are reading this book simply as a motivational guide to help people succeed in their goals, then you will see only minimal results. They may still reach their goals; but unless you are helping them tap into their unique God-given talents and spiritual gifts, they may never realize their full potential. The better they know themselves in the light of who God meant them to be, the better they will be able to move those deep anchor issues of life that keep them from moving forward. When their desires are in line with what God wants for them, their goals will not only be realized but they will be lasting and satisfying results—not just temporary fixes.

I have laid out the tools in this book to help set tangible goals, and I've outlined some strategies that will bring results for the ones you coach, but I cannot emphasize enough the importance of putting God first and understanding that He created every person as a masterpiece with a purpose to fulfill in life.

Jeremiah 29:11 (NIV)

For I know the plans I have for you," declares the Lord, "plans to prosper you and not to harm you, plans to give you hope and a future.

Understanding this concept will put every dream and goal within the realm of possibility because God is the motivating power that comes from within. When your Source of power comes from God and not from what you can do in yourself, the outcome will always be better.

Philippians 4:13 (NKJV)

I can do all things through Christ who strengthens me.

Therefore, the tools presented in this book can help those you coach to set tangible goals and use the suggested strategies to reach for the results they are after. If they understand the concept that God created them as a masterpiece with a specific purpose in mind, they can confidently set goals that will address the challenges that they face in life, whether they are physical, spiritual, financial, or mental. By putting God first and shooting the arrows of faith and the power of the Holy Spirit, they will have the necessary power to bring results that could last forever. The changes that they experience, therefore, will not be based on their own human power but rather on the power of the Holy Spirit that dwells within them.

1 Thessalonians 2:13 (NASB)

"For this reason we also constantly thank God that when you received the word of God which you heard from us, you accepted it not as the word of men, but for what it really is, the word of God, which also performs its work in you who believe."

With all, I do not negate the fact that encouraging people to move out of their comfort zones into a new place will be difficult for you or for them. Many of the issues that people deal with have been problems for them for many years, sometimes their entire lives. That is why I call it *Growing Grass on Rocks*. It isn't easy to make changes, especially when the old way has become a way of life. People in general do not like change, even when it is for their own good; and the reason it is so hard is that it may call for some sacrifices and even hardships to get to the goal. In addition, it may be just as hard for you, the coach, as it is for the one you are coaching. Both take a lot of determination and endurance.

Again, referring to Paul as he coached the Thessalonians to not give up in their Christian progress, he spoke about not only the affliction that he was going to have to endure to share these messages with people, but he was also very bothered by his fear that they would fail in shooting the arrows ahead of them. Paul knew that the tempter, the enemy, is real; and he was concerned that once he left them to function on their own that they might fall to the temptations that caused them to stumble before.

1 Thessalonians 3:4-5 (NASB)

"For indeed when we were with you, we kept telling you in advance that we were

going to suffer affliction; and so it came to pass, as you know For this reason, when I could endure it no longer, I also sent to find out about your faith, for fear that the tempter might have tempted you, and our labor would be in vain."

Later, Paul was encouraged to learn that the Thessalonians had stayed faithful and that they were shooting the arrows and seeing great success as God moved through them. You, too, will experience great successes and encouragement if you continue to diligently coach others towards their goals. As you set them up for success by helping them set their own targets and then set intermediate goals to reach those targets, they will begin to identify the obstacles that threaten their progress as they tap into the resources, they have to overcome those obstacles. At times, you may wonder if any progress is being made at all; but through the grace of God, He will use you to motivate others to shoot the arrow. Once they let it fly, you can celebrate the fact that God is using you to help someone overcome the excuses that have held them captive for so long.

They will learn to make better food choices.

They will make a schedule that creates balance in their life.

They will choose healthy relationships.

They will spend quality time with their family.

They will be confident in how God has made them.

They will be healthier.

They will make smarter money choices.

They will make church a priority.

They will get involved in service activities.

"Shoot the Arrows"

What is your target?

_____

What are 3 smaller goals to get closer to your target?

1.

_____

2.

_____

3.

_____

What will you do this week to shoot an arrow at goal 1?

_____

What will you do this week to shoot an arrow at goal 2?

_____

What will you do this week to shoot an arrow at goal 3?

What else will you do this month to shoot an arrow at goal 1?

What else will you do this month to shoot an arrow at goal 2?

What else will you do this month to shoot an arrow at goal 3?

How will you celebrate after shooting each of these arrows?

What obstacles may keep you from shooting these arrows?

How will you overcome these obstacles?

What resources do you have that could help you shoot these arrows?

Chapter 8

Analyze the Results

I was sitting in a civil engineering class as the teacher explained how to hold up a machine while another machine at the other end of the street reads the meter. Suddenly, like a lightning bolt in the sky I thought, "Can I really do this for the rest of my life?" So, I went to the college counselor and asked, "How do I change my major?" I found out that it's not that hard, and I switched my major to English because I enjoyed reading books. After sitting in my fifth class about Shakespeare I again asked myself, "What am I doing?" I'm not saying that there is anything wrong with Shakespeare, but I couldn't take it anymore; so, I switched my major to speech communication because I felt like it was an area in which I excelled. At this point, the counselor knew me very well as I asked him, "What do I have to do to just graduate because this major isn't right for me either?"

There are times in life that you may set what looks like a good target goal; but even though it may make sense to a lot of people, there may be something inside of you that says it is not right for you. That is when you must stop and analyze the targeted goal to see if the end results will produce for you what you think you want. You may even "shoot the arrows" of determination and effort with great accuracy before you realize that the results are not worth continuing in that direction.

In the last chapter, I encouraged you to make sure that the arrows you shoot reflect the concepts of putting God first and utilizing your God-given talents and spiritual gifts; otherwise, all the effort you put forth will not bring the satisfying results that you expected. Therefore, it is imperative that you know who you are in Christ; and armed with that knowledge, analyze how the perceived results will fit in with God's plan for your life.

In hindsight, I really wish I could do college over because this time I would put more focus on what God created me to be; but obviously, I can't start over. However, I can use those mistakes to help me experience a more focused future. The college degree that I ended up with is not the most effective one I could have chosen in those important years, but I believe it helped move me towards a career I really love. I have used the knowledge I gained from my first targets to refine and define the most important targets of my life more effectively. Therefore, by simply going through the process of analyzing the results you get from shooting strong arrows at your current targets, you can adjust and realign your goals as you move forward.

Human beings have a natural tendency to gravitate towards wanting to fit in and be like everyone else. In addition, many people tend to be "people pleasers" without stopping to ask God what **He** wants or even themselves what they want. This doesn't apply to everyone, of course; but you probably were told to do some things that someone else thought you should do, and you probably tried your best to do those things. Around the world, people live in societies that have expected paths and goals that everyone, for the most part, tries to move towards.

I have traveled quite a bit, and one of the things that I have noticed is how the look of our houses, cars, clothes, toys, etc. all tend to look alike based on where I am. The architecture of the homes in Paris, for example, tend to look very different than the ones in Los

Angeles; but within Paris, the homes are very similar to each other while those within Los Angeles are all very similar to each other. Each city leans toward a natural progression of personality and acceptance in which people try to achieve a certain desirable look of success that is expected in that culture. There are always a few standouts which look different; but you will notice that most of the homes, cars, clothing, toys, and etc. are all similar in architecture and design. Even in traveling within the United States from city to city, you will notice how each city has its certain areas that people desire to live in and hold up as the standard to work towards. It can be the outdoorsy style of Denver or Portland, the beach culture of Hawaii or coastal towns, or the penthouse city life of New York or Chicago.

The culture you live in has a big effect on your path of life. In addition to the general cultural expectations and traditions, you can add your family expectations and traditions that are handed down from generation to generation, including the religious training and expectations that you inherited. Then you can start to realize that you are basically hardwired or programmed to a path that has almost been chosen for you. The goals from someone in the slums of Nairobi are going to be far different than those from the elite suburbs of New York. Conversely, the target of someone who is escaping religious persecution versus the one set by a pastor's kid is going to be dramatically different in nature.

The reason that I just spent considerable time discussing your cultural and familial expectations is so that you will take a closer look at the goals you have personally set. I want you to ask yourself if they are really the targets that God has designed for your life. Perhaps those targets may be what others have said are best for you. Maybe those targets go along with something you think you want, but maybe God has something far greater for your life. Too many times we avoid really looking at our goals by resorting to catch phrases such as, "Whatever" or "That's just the way it is" or "It is what it is". Others use their families to avoid analyzing their goals when they say, "This is what's best for my family" when the truth is that they just don't want to move away from their comfort zones. The truth is that if God is not at the center of your ambitions, your family will eventually suffer the consequences; and in the final analysis, "What's best for your family" will be what God wants for you.

I would like to caution you, however, against expecting everything to turn out perfectly when you analyze the results. Hardships and struggles are naturally a part of the process of change, as we observed in the last chapter with Paul's experiences. Nevertheless, some people erroneously think that hardships and struggles are God's way of letting us know that we are on the wrong path.

As a pastor for over twenty years, I have listened to people repeatedly, usually through tears, tell me how God has closed doors in their life, an assumption they have based on the hardships and struggles they are facing—even though they believe that God had told them to take that path. One of the reasons I think these people have abandoned their goals can be traced to the "health and wealth" doctrine that has been so popular in the last thirty years. This doctrine teaches that when you are in the will of God, everything works out perfectly. Therefore, let's take a few moments to examine what the Bible really says regarding these issues.

Malachi 3:10 (NASB)

"Bring the whole tithe into the storehouse, so that there may be food in My house, and test Me now in this," says the LORD of hosts, *"if I will not open for you the windows of heaven and pour out for you a blessing until it overflows."*

This verse says that if you tithe, God will open the windows of heaven and pour out a blessing upon you until it overflows. That is exactly what it says, but I believe that the misinterpretation that the "health and wealth" doctrine proclaims has to do with the meaning of the word *blessing.* Most people in the world we live in interpret the word *blessing* to mean houses and cars, and all the trappings of a materialistic society. It means boats and airplanes and a big bank account, along with everything else you could want, including perfect health. However, when people tithe and those "blessings" don't materialize for them, they start to question God and His promises. Once again, remember that blessings are highly biased based on where you live, your family's traditions, and the culture that surrounds you. The *blessings* of the child starving in Indonesia are going to be articulated very differently than the middle-class high school student living in California. Therefore, is it possible that we might be reading into these verses something that God never intended? I think so, but let's look at one more example:

Psalm 1:1 (NASB)

"How blessed is the man who does not walk in the counsel of the wicked, Nor stand in the path of sinners, Nor sit in the seat of scoffers!"

Psalms and Proverbs are full of all these wonderful promises that if you do the right things and avoid sin, then you will be **blessed**. This is obviously very true, and you have probably experienced this many times. However, there are times when you do everything right and the world beats you down with disaster after disaster. What does that mean? Has God closed the door on you or abandoned you? Does this mean that you are walking in the counsel of the wicked and sitting in the seat of scoffers? I believe not. Other scriptures prove the fact that Christians are not exempt from hardships and struggles.

Acts 14:21-23 (NIV)

They preached the good news in that city…. strengthening the disciples and encouraging them to remain true to the faith. "We must go through many hardships to enter the kingdom of God," they said.

Romans 5:3 (NIV)

Not only so, but we also rejoice in our sufferings, because we know that suffering produces perseverance;

Jesus said this:

John 16:33 (NKJV)

These things I have spoken to you, that in Me you may have <u>peace</u>. In the world you will have tribulation; but be of good cheer, I have overcome the world."

So, what are the "blessings" that God promises when you tithe and do what is right? As you continue in the path that God has for your life, the answer to that question will become more and more abundantly clear in so many ways. That is why it is so important to know God personally, to be in touch with the Holy Spirit that is dwelling within you. To do this there are some important daily habits that you must do to make sure that you are in tune with His presence.

Seek him daily and examine his plan for you that day.

This is where my book <u>10 Steps Closer to God</u> would be of help. What I have noticed in my times of prayer each day as I ask God to guide me through the day is that I don't always hear from Him. Although I am comforted by the act of praying, I have to say that nine times out of ten I feel like my prayers go about as far as the walls of the room as I give God my list of requests for healings, jobs, relationships, and direction in how He wants to use me in my encounters and chance meetings of the day. Perhaps those prayers are answered in ways beyond my knowledge, but I don't often see much difference from my human perspective.

However, there's that tenth time when something miraculous happens that is so amazing that the only way to explain it is by the intervention of God Himself! It is truly awesome when that happens, but it doesn't happen every day. This is important to understand because if you only spend time in prayer with God about once a month, you need to think about the math. I'm not talking about the quick "Where are my keys?" kind of prayers; but rather, I'm talking about prayers of power and intensity when you are calling down the promises of God. If you only pray like that about once a month, then using the math of hearing from God about one out of ten times means that you are having an amazing experience with God maybe once or twice a year. As you think back on this last year, there was possibly a moment like this when you really felt the presence of God. It could have been when a sermon clicked at a service, or it might have happened when you were alone in the mountains, or perhaps you had a chance encounter with God when you knew it could only be Him. If you want to experience God's presence on a more consistent basis, you must increase your times with Him to include a daily time of prayer and intercession.

The second daily habit that I outline in 10 Steps Closer to God is to take the time to examine your decisions and how they affect God's Kingdom and His plan for your life.

It is important as you read the Bible and spend time in prayer that you do not adopt one single verse as your "go-to" verse for every situation. As you analyze the results of the arrows you have shot towards your goals, you may be tempted to call on that one verse and use it to validate the results of what you experienced without understanding what God is doing.   Instead, the more you understand the life of Christ and the struggles of His disciples, the better you are going to understand how God opens and closes doors. What if Paul had looked at the results of his ministry to determine whether he was on the right path? If validation had been Paul's goal, then he would certainly have looked like a total failure.

Ephesians 1:11-14 (NIV)

"In him we were also chosen, having been predestined according to the plan of him who works out everything in conformity with the purpose of his will, in order that we, who were the first to hope in Christ, might be for the praise of his glory. And you also were included in Christ when you heard the word of truth, the gospel of your salvation. Having believed, you were marked in him with a seal, the promised Holy Spirit, who is a deposit guaranteeing our inheritance until the redemption of those who are God's possession-to the praise of his glory."

In this passage, Paul proclaims that he has been predestined for the work that he is doing for God. He is on a mission to spread the incredible message of Jesus Christ from city to city. He knows that his purpose is to tell people about Christ for the glory of God; and as he shares the message of salvation, he tells them about the inheritance that they will receive and speaks of the seal of the Holy Spirit that dwells within. The ironic part of this incredible passage is that these are the very words that land Paul in prison!

If you or I had chosen the path that Paul took, we might have expected God to reward us with an outpouring of His **blessings** because of all the sacrifices we had made. Such incredible blessings would certainly validate that we had taken the right course. Paul, however, did not experience a great outpouring of miracles or blessings. Instead, he is put into prison; and as he sits there alone in his cell, you might expect him to question his path and to blame God for closing the doors of his calling, but that is not what happens.

Ephesians 6:19-20 (NIV)

"Pray also for me, that whenever I open my mouth, words may be given me so that I will fearlessly make known the mystery of the gospel, for which I am an ambassador in chains. Pray that I may declare it fearlessly, as I should."

He was an "ambassador"- someone who represents the homeland, knows the culture and the character of that homeland, and can speak of it no matter where he is sent. Under normal circumstances, an ambassador is a respected and revered person who would never be put into prison for representing his country. It would literally be an act of war to do such a thing. There could be no greater insult to a nation than to put its ambassadors to death, or even to be beaten or put into prison for any reason.

However, the homeland that Paul speaks of in this passage is not of this world; he was speaking boldly about his love for Christ given as a gift to this world. He was an ambassador for Jesus Christ; and because of his message, he is beaten, suffers all kinds of afflictions, his life is threatened, and he gets thrown into prison. As an ambassador, Paul should have experienced great privilege and respect; but instead, he faces ridicule and disrespect many times over.

How does he respond to these "closed doors" and obvious struggles against his targeted goal to obey the calling that God has put before him? He prays that when he opens his mouth, he will fearlessly preach the gospel that he has been sent to preach! It is remarkable that his prayers are not about being released or even for protection from harm. Rather, his prayers are for the wisdom and boldness to speak the mystery of the gospel no matter where he may find himself. In Paul, we see a man who has analyzed the results of his path and understands that even getting thrown into prison doesn't mean that he has missed the target! He knows what God has created him for, and he continues to be that man no matter what happens.

Paul's example is a perfect illustration of the third key habit outlined in 10 Steps Closer to God, which is to spend time getting to know the Creator and the place you represent as an "ambassador" to this world.

You cannot be an effective "ambassador" for Christ in this world if you don't really know the One Who has sent you. Therefore, it is especially imperative to analyze the results of where your path may lead.

In the natural, if a country such as the United States sent an ambassador to another country, such as China, for example, and that ambassador attempted to represent the U.S. by telling everyone that we all skip to work each day, eat Chinese food at every meal, and have trained monkeys in our homes, that person would be a very bad representative of his homeland. More than likely, he would be promptly fired for spreading lies to people who might not know any better. However, it is FAR worse to be an ambassador of Jesus Christ and know nothing about the "homeland".

I am not in any way, however, implying that you need to be a great scholar of the Bible and able to answer every question about God to be an ambassador for Christ. What I do mean is that you should make it a priority to devote some daily time in Bible study and prayer so that you can get to know God and experience the Holy Spirit dwelling within you on a more personal level.

When you spend time in Bible study and prayer, you will become a better representation of God in the world because you will know more about Who you represent! The better you know your Savior, King, and Lord, the more you will become like Him. You will be able to better analyze the results of the arrows you shoot, also, because you won't be so quick to jump to conclusions when your struggles lead to what you perceive as closed doors. In addition, you will be able to understand that not every **open** door is truly what God created you to do; it is possible that some of your decisions are based purely on the culture and traditions that have been handed down to you instead of the unique purpose for which you have been created. It is always important to closely examine the targets or goals you set to make sure that they are truly from

God. By far, your greatest example of a good "target" comes from the example of Jesus Christ.

Matthew 20:28 (NASB)

"Just as the Son of Man did not come to be served, but to serve, and to give His life a ransom for many."

When Jesus came to this earth, the world had an expectation of what God should be like and how the "Lords" of the world should hold themselves above others; but then Christ showed up and said, "No, that is not how the LORD is, and it is also not how my people will be."

Matthew 20:25-26 (NASB)

But Jesus called them to Himself and said, "You know that the rulers of the Gentiles lord it over them, and their great men exercise authority over them. 26"It is not this way among you, but whoever wishes to become great among you shall be your servant,"

Jesus was able to throw out every tradition and expectation because He knew Who He was and what He was created to do. He was also able to look past the afflictions, beatings, and death to fulfil the purpose for which He was born to do. What if Jesus had taken the scorn, the ridicule, the beatings, and the Cross as signs of closed doors? What if Jesus had taken the elders' disagreements or the religious majority's disapproval as signs of closed doors? What if Jesus had taken the threat of death as a sign of closed doors?

Do you see the point? Not every bad thing is a sign that God isn't blessing the goals you have set for yourself. You may have shot some arrows lately and experienced such negative feedback and results that you are questioning if the targets you set were really from God. It is possible that they may **not** be from God, but don't quickly assume that struggle or hardship means that God is not for you. God gave this message or something like this to each one of His disciples; and the message is for you, too, if you want to serve Jesus Christ.

Romans 1:1 (NASB)

"Paul, a bond-servant of Christ Jesus, called as an apostle, set apart for the gospel of God,"

This term *bondservant* is a special one. It means that, even though you have been given complete freedom in this world to do whatever you want, you willingly choose to give up that freedom to be a slave to your Master. It may seem a bit scary except for the fact that you know that your Master is Almighty God and that He is also your Creator Who uniquely designed you to be set apart for a great purpose. Therefore, you willingly choose to give up your worldly freedom so that you can follow His plan for your life. Ironically, the real freedom comes in trusting Him to know what is best and understanding that His plan will be far greater than your own. The Lord gave us His Word that His plan is for our good and not for our harm.

Jeremiah 29:11-14 (NIV)

For I know the plans I have for you," declares the Lord, "plans to prosper you and not to harm you, plans to give you hope and a future. 12 Then you will call upon me and come and pray to me, and I will listen to you. 13 You will seek me and find me when you seek me with all your heart.

Are you ready to be a bondservant of Christ? Are you ready to seek Him with all your heart and allow Him to direct your path? If you are, it is time to analyze the results of the arrows you have been shooting and the target/goals you have set as you move forward from point A to point B.

As you meet with the person you are trying to move from point A to point B this month (or bi-weekly), do the following:

1. Spend 5 minutes—Know the Details
2. Spend 5 minutes—Celebrate the Victories
3. Spend 5 minutes—Push through the "Noise" of the obstacles.
4. Spend 5 minutes—Build the Target (or discuss the goals set from the previous meeting), reminding them that this was the target and goals they set.
5. Spend 20 minutes—Analyze the Results with the worksheet at the end of this chapter.
6. Spend 10 minutes—Assess the Resources available to them.
7. Spend 10 minutes—Identify the Obstacles

"Analyze the Results"

What was the target you set for yourself?

_____

What were the goals you set for yourself this last month?

_____

What can you celebrate about this last month?

_____

What was an obstacle this last month?

_____

What resources did you use to overcome those obstacles?

_____

What resources do you still need to overcome those obstacles?

_____

How is your target connected to God's purpose for your life?

_____

What is unique about your target to how God has created you?

_____

How is your spiritual gift used to connect to your target?

_____

How will your target connect you to Christ?

_____

What may need to be adjusted about your target to be more in line with God's purpose and direction for your life?

_____

New Target Phrase:

What are the next three arrows that need to be shot towards your target?

1.

_____

_____

_____

2.

_____

_____

_____

3.

_____

_____

_____

When will you shoot these arrows, what is your timeline to complete these arrows, and how will you celebrate these victories?

Target 1.

Target 2.

Target 3.

Chapter 9

Re-define Your Target

Michelangelo once said, "The greater danger for most of us is not that our aim is too high and we miss it, but that it is too low, and we reach it." Thus, setting small targets may be easy to reach, but there may be a much bigger goal that God has in mind for you. There is a good chance that the person you are coaching started out with a target that was easily attained within the first two months. In fact, you may have played a part in encouraging your person to aim low in order that, not only they would feel successful, but that you, too, might feel validated as a good coach.

Most of the time, many people just seem to live day to day with some vague desire or dream to do something big in the future, but they have no real plan on how to get there. "Growing grass on rocks" is simply a figurative term for helping a person move from where they are to where they need or want to be; and by this time, I hope that you can see the value of what you are doing and how powerful it is to move someone out of their comfort zones into areas of new growth and fulfilled dreams.

An interesting thing that I have observed is that when a person sets a clear target in life and then defines clear goals to reach that target, there is something that kicks in internally that causes that person to be completely motivated in mind, body, and spirit to reach their target. Therefore, once you have picked someone to coach, and they have agreed to be part of the process, it follows that their internal drive will usually kick in; and they will seriously take off at full speed to reach their goal. It is then, while excitement is high, that you want to encourage them to think big and reach for what they really and truly want. At this point in your training, you know that God has not called you to aim for small targets in life. Instead, He has created you in His image; and as you look through the Bible, you always see Him calling His people to do great exploits and to aim for big targets.

In this chapter, we will look at a variety of great people from the Bible who had to re-define and re-adjust their personal goals and targets to fit what God wanted for them before they were able to do the great exploits that we read about— people such as Noah, Abraham, Moses, Joshua, David, Esther, Job, and Jeremiah, as well as many Major and Minor prophets.

Noah

Genesis 6:13 (NASB)

"Then God said to Noah, 'The end of all flesh has come before Me; for the earth is filled with violence because of them; and behold, I am about to destroy them with the earth.'"

How would you like to be called to build a gigantic boat when you have no training as an engineer; and the boat is supposed to protect you and your family from something called "rain" that you've never seen or heard of before? Sometimes the targets that God calls you to hit will take you far from your comfort zone, and other people may think you are crazy. You may be ridiculed by all of society, including your family and friends, because your dream is so farfetched in their natural minds. However, if you are confident in your relationship with God and in the mission that He has given you, you will understand that you are an "ambassador" in a foreign land and that you will be willing, if necessary, to re-define your goals and adjust them to the God-sized target that God has for you.

What is your God-sized targets regarding your finances?

What is your God-sized targets regarding your body?

What is your God-sized targets regarding your career?

What is your God-sized targets regarding your time?

What is your God-sized targets regarding your relationships?

What is your God-sized targets regarding your personal growth?

What is your God-sized targets with God?

Abram

Genesis 12:1-3 (NASB)

"Now the LORD said to Abram, "Go forth from your country And from your relatives And from your father's house, To the land which I will show you; And I will make you a great nation, And I will bless you, And make your name great; And so you shall be a blessing; And I will bless those who bless you, And the one who curses you I will curse. And in you all the families of the earth will be blessed."

When God called Abram, Abram was in a comfortable place; his home and his finances were in pretty good shape. Then God ordered him to pick up everything, leave his country, and all his relatives so that he could go to a place that God said He would eventually show him. I'm sure that Abram must have said, "I'm sorry, God, but what did You say?" Abram's story prompts us to look at where we are in different areas of our life, areas that we may need to give more attention to in order that we are ready when God gives us a big assignment! This is what I'm calling "re-defining" or "re-adjusting" the target. Sometime what we want and what God wants is not the same thing, and we must adjust our steps to get in line with his.

For example, perhaps your finances have been a hindrance to God's plan for your life (whether that be rich or poor). Maybe it is time to pray about where you are living, what you are doing, and how you are saving (or not saving) to re-define your target.

Moses

Exodus 3:10-12 (NASB)

"Therefore, come now, and I will send you to Pharaoh, so that you may bring

My people, the sons of Israel, out of Egypt.' But Moses said to God, 'Who am I, that I should go to Pharaoh, and that I should bring the sons of Israel out of Egypt?' And He said, 'Certainly I will be with you, and this shall be the sign to you that it is I who have sent you: when you have brought the people out of Egypt, you shall worship God at this mountain.'"

Moses had been away from Egypt for many years. He had started a new life and most likely had no ambitions to go back. Then God gave Moses a new target that was far bigger than anything he had ever done before, a target that took him from the life he thought he had carved out for himself.

You may have to encourage the ones you coach to look at their targets in the light of where they are with their careers, personal growth, and relationships and make sure that they are focused on the path that God has planned for them. Career choices are often chosen based on what is most desirable in the culture one lives in; and personal growth targets usually end up being more like a "self-help book" to advance one's career instead of drawing closer to God. Relationships, too, are often based on what will benefit oneself more than what will be pleasing to God.

Therefore, as you coach others toward their goals, it is imperative that you ask them some important questions, such as the following: **What if your plan is different from the one God has for you?** What if God has a plan to send you to help a group of people who aren't going to be happy to see you, like the plan He had for Moses? What if the career you desire is different from the path that God wants you to take? What if personal growth means that God wants you to go to a foreign land to learn a new language and a new culture so that you can plant the first seeds of Christ with a new group of people?

Of course, it is highly possible that those you lead will have plans that fall exactly in line with God's plan for their lives; but it is always worthwhile to take some time now and again to look closely at the targets to make sure that they are big enough to fit God-sized miracles. Then, if necessary, you can help them re-define and re-adjust their targets so that they stay in line with what God wants.

Joshua

Joshua 1:1-7 (NASB)

"Now it came about after the death of Moses the servant of the LORD, that the LORD spoke to Joshua the son of Nun, Moses' servant, saying, 'Moses My servant is dead; now therefore arise, cross this Jordan, you and all this

people, to the land which I am giving to them, to the sons of Israel. 'Every place on which the sole of your foot treads, I have given it to you, just as I spoke to Moses. 'From the wilderness and this Lebanon, even as far as the great river, the river Euphrates, all the land of the Hittites, and as far as the Great Sea toward the setting of the sun will be your territory. 'No man will be able to stand before you all the days of your life. Just as I have been with Moses, I will be with you; I will not fail you or forsake you. 'Be strong and courageous, for you shall give this people possession of the land which I swore to their fathers to give them. 'Only be strong and very courageous; be careful to do according to all the law which Moses My servant commanded you; do not turn from it to the right or to the left, so that you may have success wherever you go."

When God called Joshua and gave him the target plan, He had in mind, it was big enough to scare an entire nation of people. According to God's plan, they would soon face Jericho, a powerhouse city surrounded by massive walls. Heretofore, the goals they had dealt with were minor and insignificant compared to taking down the walls of Jericho! What must have gone through their minds as God revealed his target to them, as well as his plans for all the other cities and armies that they were going to face?

Although the targets that you may be helping others, as well as yourself, to reach may seem like nothing in comparison to those that Moses and Joshua were given, they are the same. We don't always fight against things that we can see such as taking down physical cities, but we do fight battles on a different plane.

Ephesians 6:12 NIV

For our struggle is not against flesh and blood, but against the rulers, against the authorities, against the powers of this dark world and against the spiritual forces of evil in the heavenly realms.

For example, let's look at a different kind of physical battle that many people describe as their target goal—losing weight. You, as their coach, may know that the weight loss target is not the ultimate target that God wants; but your person must be coached to re-define and re-adjust to see that. At first glance, it may not seem like a spiritual thing in the least. However, if a person's excess weight keeps him or her from doing the bigger job that God has called him to do, then it is a definite roadblock to ultimate success with God's true plan for them. This is when you, as the coach, can help them re-define their goals to continue to make progress toward the big thing God wants. When a person can see something bigger ahead than the immediate struggle, it may give them the impetus to meet the smaller intermediate goal of losing the weight, for example, on the way to ultimate success. Thus, the weight loss target that they may have had won't seem as difficult as the new calling from God.

In the weight loss scenario, it is your job as a person's coach to help them see why losing weight is a spiritual battle. The questions you want them to answer are these: "Why do you want a better, healthier, stronger body?" "What could you do for God with a dynamic body ready for action?" Thus, you can help them to re-define their target so that they can see what they will be able to accomplish for God with their new body instead of just simply losing weight. This kind of leading can be adapted to any number of physical, or professional, or relational problems. Once a person can see the big picture of what God wants for their life, they can re-define their target to see past the day-to-day struggles.

David

1 Samuel 17:37 (NASB)

"And David said, 'The LORD who delivered me from the paw of the lion and from the paw of the bear, He will deliver me from the hand of this Philistine.' And Saul said to David, 'Go, and may the LORD be with you.'"

When David set out to re-define the target in which God wanted to use him to defeat a nation and inspire another, the strategy he used was that of taking the time to remember all the ways that God had been with him in the past. Sometimes the people you coach gets so bogged down in the present struggle that they cannot even see where they are going. However, just as David recounted all the smaller victories that God had given him—delivering him from the paw of the lion and the paw of the bear—you can help your person recount what God has done for them. God calls us to do big-sized things, but He gives us smaller victories along the way to remind us that He has always been there when we grow weary or scared of what lies ahead. You will be amazed at how rejuvenating it is when a person realizes how many things God has done that they have forgotten about or even things they didn't even notice. Remembering what God has done in the past will help catapult people to the God-sized targets ahead, and those times of remembering turn into times of victory and celebration.

Esther

Esther 4:13-14 (NASB)

"Then Mordecai told them to reply to Esther, 'Do not imagine that you in the king's palace can escape any more than all the Jews. 'For if you remain silent at this time, relief and deliverance will arise for the Jews from another place and you and your father's house will perish. And who knows whether you have not attained royalty for such a time as this?'"

For such a time as this! Esther didn't want to approach the King because it could mean her death. Esther was in the King's palace being treated as royalty after a long process and struggle to get there; but just getting to be queen was not God's target for Esther. The target goal God had in mind was much bigger, and it could cost her everything. She really didn't want to be queen at all, but she realized that maybe God had put her in that place at that time for "such a time as this," which was a time when her Jewish people needed to be saved. She was at the right place at the right time.

The person you are and the person you are leading from point A to point B is also unique and special to this time on earth and this place in time. Only they live in the neighborhood they live in, work at the job they work at, have the influence that they have and so forth. We do not know all the ways of God, but we know that He uses people as part of His perfect plan; and it is your job to help the ones you coach to realize their once-in-a-lifetime position to do far more than what they first thought possible. It is your job to help them re-define their target for the position and place where they are in history and life.

Job

Job 1:8-12 (NASB)

"The LORD said to Satan, 'Have you considered My servant Job? For there is no one like him on the earth, a blameless and upright man, fearing God and turning away from evil." Then Satan answered the LORD, 'Does Job fear God for nothing? 'Have You not made a hedge about him and his house and all that he has, on every side? You have blessed the work of his hands, and his possessions have increased in the land. 'But put forth Your hand now and touch all that he has; he will surely curse You to Your face.' Then the LORD said to Satan, 'Behold, all that he has is in your power, only do not put forth your hand on him.' So Satan departed from the presence of the LORD."

Job had no idea that a spiritual battle was being played out in the heavens.

Job had no idea that his story would be recorded and read for thousands of years to come. Job had no idea that the events of his life would inspire millions of people who would face the hardest situations that humans would ever have to face. All these things were true about Job and the legacy that he left; and they could be true of the life you are moving, as well. You don't always know what God is doing, so you need to press into Him even more to make sure that your targets are lining up with His plans.

Jeremiah

Jeremiah 1:5-10 (NASB)

"'Before I formed you in the womb I knew you, and *before you were born, I consecrated you; I have appointed you a prophet to the nations.' Then I said, 'Alas, Lord GOD! Behold, I do not know how to speak, Because I am a youth.' But the LORD said to me, 'Do not say, 'I am a youth,' Because everywhere I send you, you shall go, and all that I command you, you shall speak. 'Do not be afraid of them, For I am with you to deliver you,' declares the LORD. Then the LORD stretched out His hand and touched my mouth, and the LORD said to me, 'Behold, I have put My words in your mouth. 'See, I have appointed you this day over the nations and over the kingdoms, to pluck up and to break down, to destroy and to overthrow, To build and to plant.'"*

Jeremiah is one of the many Major and Minor Prophets who we could talk about in this chapter as an inspiration to help people re-define their targets. Each prophet had to be reminded that God knew them in the womb and set them apart to be His voice to their lost generation. Each one was called to do something bigger than themselves, and most had to face incredible sacrifices and ridicule to be the hands and feet of God in their world.

It is the same with the ones you will be leading. Just as many of the prophets and disciples of Bible times gave up family businesses and the lives they were accustomed to in order to follow Jesus, the ones you lead may have to experience some sacrifices, as well, if they want to follow the path God has chosen for them. They may have to set new targets in the areas of their finances, in their physical bodies, in their professional lives, in their time management, in their relationships, and in their personal growth to reach their target goals. The greatest example we can look at, of course, is Jesus Christ Himself who was offered all the kingdoms of the world; but He knew God's plan was greater, and He knew what His purpose was. He pursued the target that God wanted for His life to save all mankind from Hell.

So, what excuses can people bring before God when it comes to the targets they need to set for their lives? There is nothing that He hasn't shown us clearly in Scripture through the many examples throughout the Bible. Over and over, we are shown that His plans are far greater than ours and that He can do even greater things than we can imagine. It is up to us to now re-define the targets we have set for ourselves, as well as for the ones we are helping and make sure that we have set them big enough for God-sized miracles to happen. As you re-define your targets, I would encourage you to ponder some of the words that God spoke about the last days and then the words that Jesus spoke before He went back to Heaven, words in which he admonished us to press on after the Holy Spirit has come.

Acts 2:17-21 (NASB)

"'And it shall be in the last days,' God says, 'That I will pour forth of My Spirit on all mankind; And your sons and your daughters shall prophesy, And your young men shall see visions, And your old men shall dream dreams; Even on My bondslaves, both men and women, I will in those days pour forth of My spirit And they shall prophesy. 'And I will grant wonders in the sky above And signs on the earth below, Blood, and fire, and vapor of smoke. 'The sun will be turned into darkness And the moon into blood, Before the great and glorious day of the Lord shall come. 'And it shall be that everyone who calls on the name of the Lord will be saved.'"

Mark 16:15-18 (NASB)

"And He said to them, 'Go into all the world and preach the gospel to all creation. 'He who has believed and has been baptized shall be saved; but he

who has disbelieved shall be condemned. 'These signs will accompany those who have believed: in My name they will cast out demons, they will speak with new tongues; they will pick up serpents, and if they drink any deadly poison, it will not hurt them; they will lay hands on the sick, and they will recover.'"

Matthew 29:18-20 (NASB)

"And Jesus came up and spoke to them, saying, 'All authority has been given to Me in heaven and on earth. 'Go therefore and make disciples of all the nations, baptizing them in the name of the Father and the Son and the Holy Spirit, teaching them to observe all that I commanded you; and lo, I am with you always, even to the end of the age.'"

I would imagine that the targets that you have set for yourself and for those you have helped to set are not nearly as strong in language as the above scriptures. After the Holy Spirit came, God expected us to do all the things that He says we could do—prophesy, see visions, cast out demons, make disciples of people, and so forth. Do you believe this? Do you believe that when the Creator of the universe, God Himself, dwells within you as the Holy Spirit that there is nothing that you can't do? The fact is that we need to believe these things!

Therefore, it is time to re-define the targets in those you are leading, as well as for us, into God-sized targets that probably won't happen in a month or two without a miracle from God. We were designed to go after goals with the voracity of a lion chasing after their prey. This is why the person you are moving from point A to point B should be reaching new goals in every month that you meet. It is exciting to watch! However, it is time now to move them into goals that are much larger and will have life-changing results in the kingdom of God.

Revelation 1:1-3 (NASB)

"The Revelation of Jesus Christ, which God gave Him to show to His bond-servants, the things which must soon take place; and He sent and communicated it by His angel to His bond-servant John, who testified to the word of God and to the testimony of Jesus Christ, even to all that he saw. Blessed is he who reads and those who hear the words of the prophecy, and heed the things which are written in it; for the time is near."

Revelation 22:18-21 (NASB)

"I testify to everyone who hears the words of the prophecy of this book: if anyone adds to them, God will add to him the plagues which are written in this book; and if anyone takes away from the words of the book of this prophecy, God

will take away his part from the tree of life and from the holy city, which are written in this book. He who testifies to these things says, 'Yes, I am coming quickly.' Amen. Come, Lord Jesus. The grace of the Lord Jesus be with all. Amen."

As the book of Revelation ends, we are reminded that we are in the last days on earth. Our King is returning, and it will be a surprise to those who aren't watching for His coming. We are watching and believing that God is powerful and moving daily.

God wants you to have a daily relationship with His children, and He wants to pour out blessings on their lives. His sons and daughters sometimes get these blessings mixed up with the blessings of our culture; but, nevertheless, God is still working. Take some time to re-examine the life goals and targets of the person you are helping grow, and make sure that those goals and targets are working with the plans of the Holy Spirit dwelling within them.

As you meet with the person you are trying to move from point A to point B this month (or bi-weekly), do the following:

1. Spend 5 minutes—Know the Details
2. Spend 5 minutes—Celebrate the Victories
3. Spend 5 minutes—Push through the "Noise" of obstacles.
4. Spend 5 minutes—Build the Target (or discuss the goals they set in the previous meeting), reminding them that this was their target and goals.
5. Spend 10 minutes—Analyze the Results
6. Spend 20 minutes—Re-define the Target (Use the worksheet at the end of the chapter)

7. Spend 10 minutes—Assess the Resources available to them.
8. Spend 10 minutes—Identify the Obstacles

Re-define Your Target

What is your target when it comes to finances?

_____

What is your target when it comes to health?

_____

What is your target when it comes to your career?

_____

What is your target when it comes to time?

_____

What is your target with all the relationships of your life?

_____

What is your target when it comes to personal growth?

_____

What is your target when it comes to God?

_____

What are 3 goals to reach your target in each of the above categories?

_____
_____
_____
_____
_____

What will be the obstacles in each of those areas?

_____

_____

_____

_____

_____

What are some of the resources you need to overcome those obstacles?

_____

_____

_____

What resources do you still need to overcome those obstacles?

_____

_____

_____

How can you brainstorm to reach those resources?

_____

_____

_____

How will you celebrate each time you reach a new goal?

_____

_____

_____

Chapter 10

Shoot Again

I have noticed something interesting about human beings. Overall, people talk about their goals, ideas, projects, analyzing, planning, organizing, and strategies all the time; but only very few do those things. It seems to take a special kind of person who will go through the process of doing something with the understanding that it might be an epic failure and do it anyway. Abraham Lincoln once said, "Things may come to those who wait, but only the things left by those who hustle." Personally, I don't like getting the leftovers, and I don't like wasting time just waiting on something to happen, either. I have worked for some time now, and I am amazed at how much time is wasted in meetings where there is a whole lot of talk about all the things that are wrong and all the things that need improvement when the truth is that, if just one person would get up and start doing something, there would be no more need for a meeting. I usually spend most of my time in those meetings just trying to figure out who are there to talk and who are there to work.

Life is hard, and it takes a lot of work to be successful; and I have noticed that other people are drawn to those who achieve any level of success. I have found that the more problems you solve and the more things you overcome, the more highly sought after you will be. In general, people are looking for those who get things done, not for those who only talk about what needs to be done; the truth is that anyone can diagnose the problems. As a pastor, I am approached daily by people who have complaints about the way things are being done; but it is very seldom that anyone says, "I'm ready to work, what needs to be done?"

Therefore, I want to encourage you to train and empower those whom you lead to be doers rather than talkers, people who get things done! As you go through the process of moving people from point A to point B, they may take a few steps forward and then a step backwards. However, as their coach, it is your job to not let them get stuck when that happens. You want to keep them moving forward, and that is the focus of this chapter. You want to impress upon those you coach that not everything that they attempt will work out perfectly. In fact, some things will be a complete failure; but the idea is to learn from the mistakes, make the necessary corrections, if possible, and "shoot again". That simply means to give it another try, and don't give up.

You must reassure those you coach that perfection is not the goal. In fact, most new endeavors are messy and may require multiple attempts to get started, especially when the endeavor involves something that they have never tried before or are not familiar with. A lot of people wait around their entire lives for someone or something to inspire them to move before they do anything, and they are the ones who usually end up never having accomplished anything at all. That euphoric moment that they wait for never comes; and five years later, they're still in the same place—still waiting on something to happen. However, when the inspiration comes from God, they won't be dependent on some outside force to motivate them to move forward.

I would advise you to have the ones that you work with to write down exactly what they would like to accomplish and where they see themselves in five years. You can show them the form at the end of Chapter Nine where they can write specific goals in every major area of their lives; the more specific the better. Let them know that they can move forward and do what God has inspired them to do without getting someone else's permission or reassurance.

No one else is going to do the work that God has specifically designed them to do, and neither can they afford to wait for someone else to change before they move forward. The boss, the children, the parents, friends, spouse, colleagues, or anyone else will probably not make any significant changes, so they will have to move forward without expecting others to pave their way to success. Hopefully, the ones you are coaching have had the opportunity to re-define and re-adjust their goals, and they know that they are the only ones who can shoot the arrow again. Other people do not determine their success, and other people cannot make the necessary changes to ensure their success.

Some people like to conveniently blame others for their lack of progress—their spouses, their kids, the leadership team at church, their parents, and on and on when they are the ones to blame. Usually, it is the fear of risk or failure that prevents a person from making a change; but risk will always be part of change making, and failure will always be a possibility. There may even be some danger involved when you move from a comfortable safe place to a place that God has designed for you. When you look at the examples of people in the Bible who were called to do great things for God, you will notice that great risks and dangers were almost always part of the deal. You must make the point with those you coach that the path will probably not be easy, but the rewards will outweigh the risks. In addition, you have impressed upon them the probability of obstacles getting in the way and have warned them that frustrations and pain go hand in hand with the obstacles and tragedies of life. Therefore, it is time to let go of the excuses and trepidations and just shoot again.

Struggle is a part of life, whether you move forward or stand still. Sometimes it's a struggle just to get out of bed in the morning, so you might as well be making progress! For a moment, let's look at the struggle it takes to be an athlete, especially the ones who make it to the Olympics. They did not get there without much struggle, determination, and perseverance. They made it there through a lot of sacrifice, sweat, pain, and tears; it took a lot of hard work to get there. For true athletes, failure is not in their vocabulary. They don't say things like, "Yesterday, I couldn't overcome that height, that time, or that

distance, so it must not be meant to be."
No, by the time an athlete has reached
the point where others are willing to pay
to watch them perform, failure is not an
option. They may experience failure
from time to time, but they do not stay in
that place; it's not the end of their story.
Instead, they look at the obstacle or the
failure, they learn something from it,
they re-define and make the necessary
adjustments, and then they try again. It
is the natural progression towards
ultimate success for athletes, and that
same progression will work for the ones
you coach, as well.

Paul used the analogy of runners who
run for a prize to show us that we, too,
must be single-minded towards the
goals we set. In the case of setting
goals, the target you set is the prize;
and you do not want to be half-hearted
and lethargic about shooting the arrows.
You want to win the prize!

1 Corinthians 9:24-27 (NIV)

Do you not know that in a race all the runners run, but only one gets the prize? Run in such a way as to get the prize. 25 Everyone who competes in the games goes into strict training. They do it to get a crown that will not last; but we do it to get a crown that will last forever. 26 Therefore I do not run like a man running aimlessly; I do not fight like a man beating the air. 27 No, I beat my body and make it my slave so that after I have preached to others, I myself will not be disqualified for the prize.

Philippians 3:12-14 (NASB)

"Not that I have already obtained it or have already become perfect, but I press on so that I may lay hold of that for which also I was laid hold of by Christ Jesus. Brethren, I do not regard myself as having laid hold of it yet; but one thing I do: forgetting what lies

behind and reaching forward to what lies ahead, I press on toward the goal for the prize of the upward call of God in Christ Jesus."

It is important to remind those you are leading that God knew what He was getting when He called them to do His work; and He already knows that they are not perfect just as none of us are. You must also remind them that the prize they are pressing towards is the target goal that they themselves set at the very beginning of this "growing grass on rocks" process. As they have accomplished the smaller intermediate steps towards their bigger targeted goals, they have been able to remove some deep-seated anchors that held them in one place. Then, as they have moved on to new levels, the enemy once again has presented them with unexpected obstacles. It has been your job as their leader to continually remind them that obstacles don't equal failures.

Just as it is not a sin to be tempted, it is also not a failure to come up against obstacles. The fact is that everyone comes up against obstacles in life, but you want to present them as mere "bumps" in the road. The "bumps" may slow them down for a moment, but they don't stop them from making progress. You want to inspire those you coach to learn from their mistakes, re-group, restructure, and tweak where needed, and then shoot the arrow again.

As they take aim and shoot again, you will be able to celebrate the victories from the past, push through the noise of distractions, and build a better target. Then, as they look at their target, they can calculate the resources that are available to them and identify the obstacles as they come up. Together, you and the ones you lead can analyze the results from the past arrows they shot and help them re-define the target as they shoot again.

All these reminders may appear to be generated by human power until you remember that nothing is possible without utilizing the powerful gift of the Holy Spirit that dwells inside. It is the most valuable resource that a person has available; and it is imperative that you coach your person to be open and receptive to listening to the voice of the Holy Spirit because that is what empowers them to do things that they would not be able to accomplish in their own power.

As you are "growing grass on rocks", I encourage you to share the vastness and awesomeness of the gift of the Holy Spirit to the ones you want to inspire. As you move people from point A to point B, never let them forget about this wonderful gift that dwells within them; for many people, it is an untapped resource that they don't even know they have! You can give all kinds of information and instruction on how to move forward towards a goal; but without including the Holy Spirit as being the most valuable Source of power, reaching the goal will not bring the happiness or satisfaction that it promised to bring. Being in tune with the Holy Spirit is the only true Source of satisfaction. This gift allows them to go beyond themselves and move past the many obstacles that come along the way.

In the remainder of this last chapter, I want to explore and articulate what exactly this gift is and how it works within us. Paul gives us a clear path to understanding this gift:

Ephesians 3:14-17 (NASB)

"For this reason I bow my knees before the Father, from whom every family in heaven and on earth derives its name, that He would grant you, according to the riches of His glory, to be

strengthened with power through His Spirit in the inner man, so that Christ may dwell in your hearts through faith…"

This is the second time Paul prayed in Ephesians; the first prayer in chapter one was for enlightenment, but the second prayer is for enablement.

In this passage, Paul prays that they would somehow wrap their heads around the awesome power that they had available to them through the Holy Spirit, which they had dwelling within them. He is saying that nothing would be impossible for them, regardless of the purpose and plan that God had for them, if they would learn to tap into this amazing Resource.

This message is for you and the ones you are leading, as well. God wants you to experience and then share with others the incredible power of the Holy Spirit and how, by tapping into this power, they will experience a deep contentment, excitement, and passion that will be more than they ever dreamed possible. Prayer is the way to tap into this power. Therefore, personal prayer needs to be a daily priority for those you are leading. As their coach, you should want them to be so empowered by the Holy Spirit that they will find that passionate excitement that will propel them into a deep personal relationship with their Heavenly Father. Then, just as Paul assured his audience in the passage above, what they experience will surpass (go far beyond) any earthly knowledge that they may have as they are filled with God's Holy Spirit.

Ephesians 3:18-22 (NASB)

"...and that you, being rooted and grounded in love, may be able to comprehend with all the saints what is the breadth and length and height and depth, 19 and to know the love of Christ which surpasses knowledge, that you

may be filled up to all the fullness of God." Now to Him who is able to do far more abundantly beyond all that we ask or think, according to the power that works within us, to Him be the glory in the church and in Christ Jesus to all generations forever and ever. Amen."

Thus, as you help people "shoot again," you can inspire them to do it with strength because they are empowered by the Holy Spirit.

Acts 1:8 (NASB)

"but you will receive power when the Holy Spirit has come upon you; and you shall be My witness both in Jerusalem, and in all Judea and Samaria, and even to the remotest part of the earth."

Jesus performed his ministry on the earth through the power of the Holy Spirit. Acts Chapter Two is the beginning of the Church Age, the age in which we now live. There are fifty-nine references to the Spirit in the Book of

Acts, which is about one-fourth of all the references mentioned in the New Testament. When the Church Age began, it was built by the power of the Holy Spirit working through ordinary people just like you and me, including those that you are leading right now. Every person is very capable of finding incredible strength to do great things for Christ, simply by utilizing and tapping into the Holy Spirit which dwells inside of every believer.

Thinking about the great power of the Holy Spirit reminds me of a huge dam called Millerton Dam, which is near where I lived as a child. I remember looking at the water spilling over the top of the dam during the summer months, and I just assumed that the power came from what I could see. Later, however, I learned that what I saw spilling over the top of the dam was just the extra froth, the overflow. The real power of the dam, I learned, comes from deep inside the workings of the dam; there are turbines and generators transforming the tons and tons of water into electricity—quietly, without notice, not like the flashy froth on top.

The Holy Spirit works in much the same way. Its power Source comes from deep inside of the believer, quietly doing His work without notice but slowly transforming the believer into something powerful in the kingdom of God. However, people in general are often more impressed with what they can see on the outside, so they look for things that are more impressive to the human mind—the flashy or frothy sorts of manifestations that may not necessarily prove anything at all. Some things may look good and feel good; but unless they are fueled by the power of the Holy Spirit, they won't have lasting results. God wants us to be impressed with the fruit of the Holy Spirit—love, joy, peace, patience, goodness, gentleness, kindness, faithfulness, and self-control. Bearing fruit is the evidence of being filled with the Holy Spirit, and real power comes from inside of ordinary people who have been commissioned by the power of the Holy Spirit. You may be extremely satisfied when the person you are working with reaches his or her target quickly; but ultimately, it is the Holy Spirit that does the work in that person. Notice Paul's prayers from prison in Colossians:

Colossians 1:9-12 (NASB)

"We have not ceased to pray for you and to ask that you may be filled with the knowledge of His will in all spiritual wisdom and understanding, so that you will walk in a manner worthy of the Lord, to please Him in all respects, bearing fruit in every good work and increasing in the knowledge of God; strengthened with all power, according to His glorious might, for the attaining of all steadfastness and patience; joyously."

Once again, Paul is in prayer while in prison. He is not praying for escape, but rather for the knowledge to walk in a manner worthy of the Lord. Have you helped those you are working with to set targets worthy of the Lord? Then you can expect to see great results because of the Holy Spirit that dwells within.

In this chapter, I have touched on how people devote much time and attention to the development of their physical bodies because this is something that most people can relate to. I pointed out that the fact that athletes and runners have been used to teach spiritual truths as far back as Bible days, again because people understand that analogy. Therefore, with that in mind, I will end this chapter by again making a comparison of the physical with the spiritual to show you that discipline is extremely fundamental in reaching your goals in life. It takes discipline to keep moving towards a target, especially when you must shoot again!

Why do people work out and fill the gyms daily when it's so hard to do? It causes pain and requires consistent discipline to keep their bodies in good shape, but they do it to look good and to add longevity to their lives. However, those who are truly successful also realize that they must add a healthy diet to their daily workouts, as well. Diet and exercise go together, and they both take a lot of discipline. Discipline calls for doing things that can be a struggle and can be difficult; and, in addition, you must make time to accomplish your desired goal.

Most people understand clearly what it takes to reach a physical goal, but few people truly get the connection of discipline when it comes to their spiritual goals. Yet, the development of your spiritual man is far more important than the development of the physical body.

The body will pass away no matter how much time and effort you put into staying in good shape, but the spiritual will live forever. That is why it is far more important to put your focus on the disciplines of prayer and Bible study and staying connected to the power of the Holy Spirit.

Spiritual goals require just as much discipline as anything else; but the real beauty of staying spiritually healthy is that the time you devote to prayer and Bible study will last forever. Staying in good spiritual shape will give you the power and strength required to shoot again at the targets that God has designed specifically for you to reach. If you will stay focused on the process outlined in this book, I can assure you that you will see incredible results. Therefore, I encourage you to "Shoot Again" with the power of the Holy Spirit behind you. You can read about it, talk about it, even write about it; but at some point, you will have to just step up and do it! Shoot again!

As you meet with the person you are trying to move from point A to point B this month (or bi-weekly), do the following:

1. Spend 5 minutes—Know the Details
2. Spend 5 minutes—Celebrate the Victories
3. Spend 5 minutes—Push through the "Noise" of distractions.
4. Spend 10 minutes—Build the Target (go over the goals from the last meeting and what progress was made)
5. Spend 5 minutes—Analyze the Results
6. Spend 5 minutes—Re-define the Target.
7. Spend 5 minutes—Assess the Resources available to them.
8. Spend 5 minutes—Identify the Obstacles

9. Spend 15 minutes—Shoot Again! Take the time to remind them of the power of the Holy Spirit dwelling within them as you do the worksheet at the end of this chapter.

"What Else?"

Matthew 7:24-27 (NASB)

"Therefore everyone who hears these words of Mine and acts on them, may be compared to a wise man who built his house on the rock. 'And the rain fell, and the floods came, and the winds blew and slammed against that house; and yet it did not fall, for it had been founded on the rock. 'Everyone who hears these words of Mine and does not act on them, will be like a foolish man who built his house on the sand. 'The rain fell, and the floods came, and the winds blew and slammed against that house; and it fell—and great was its fall."

It is Time to Shoot Again!

What is your target?

_____

How is this target empowered by the Holy Spirit?

_____

How are you uniquely designed and called by God for this target?

_____

What are 3 goals that will move you towards this target?

1.

_____

2.

_____

3.

_____

What are some of the obstacles that will challenge you in these goals?

1.

_____

2.

_____

3.

_____

What are some resources to help you overcome these obstacles?

1.

_____

2.

_____

3.

_____

_____

How will you celebrate as you reach these goals?

Made in the USA
Columbia, SC
31 October 2024

45194027R00152